D0873564

She Was Healed

Shanda Tripp

with contributions by
Edith Tripp and Hannah Tripp

TRILOGY CHRISTIAN PUBLISHERS
Tustin, CA

Trilogy Christian Publishers
A Wholly Owned Subsidiary of Trinity Broadcasting Network
2442 Michelle Drive
Tustin, CA 92780

She Was Healed

Rights Department, 2442 Michelle Drive, Tustin, CA 92780.

Trilogy Christian Publishing/TBN and colophon are trademarks of Trinity Broadcasting Network.

For information about special discounts for bulk purchases, please contact Trilogy Christian Publishing.

Trilogy Disclaimer: The views and content expressed in this book are those of the author and may not necessarily reflect the views and doctrine of Trilogy Christian Publishing or the Trinity Broadcasting Network.

Manufactured in the United States of America

10 9 8 7 6 5 4 3 2 1

Library of Congress Cataloging-in-Publication Data is available.

ISBN: 978-1-68556-965-5

E-ISBN: 978-1-68556-966-2 (ebook)

To say that Laurie and I, along with our entire family, have been close to the Tripp family over multiple decades would be an understatement. When ministering through song on TBN, my father would always request his favorite written by LaVerne: "We'll Not Be Defeated." That's not unlike the running theme of three generations of valiant Tripp women. Like the persistent woman with the "issue of blood" in the Scriptures, each of them has had to push through remarkable challenges to get to Jesus—where their miracle breakthrough was waiting!

—Matt & Laurie Crouch
President, Trinity Broadcasting Network

This book is just what you need to realize that God is NEVER done with us. This book is full of HOPE. As long as you have a pulse, God has a plan! It's time to get back up and keep moving forward!

—Real Talk Kim
Pastor, author, speaker

The best way to write a book is to have lived it. We have been friends with the Tripp family for decades, and we became especially close when we moved to their town in 2012. Not only Laverne and his sons, but also their wives and daughters, have become pillars to so many through their faithfulness to God as pastors and singers. They have persevered through the worst of circumstances. They have remained steady in a shifting world. They have loved the unlovable and given more than they had to give. Their stories will heal you, inspire you, and compel you to keep pressing through the crowd to Jesus, no matter how impossible it may seem. We love these ladies—and you will, too.

—The Isaacs
Opry Members—bluegrass & Southern
gospel music legends

Here are three generations of godly examples of Proverbs 31 women. I am blessed to call Shanda Tripp my pastor. I have watched her live her life with faith in the promises that are found in the Bible. After her dear husband, Pastor Robb Tripp, went to be with the Lord, Pastor Shanda continued to be a mother, shepherd her flock at The Fire Place Fellowship in Tennessee, work tirelessly for foster children, and provide for her missions in Haiti with a joy and strength that can only come from a strong relationship with Jesus Christ. I highly recommend this book.

—Charlene Tilton
Actress/television icon

There are very few people who affect everyone around them, and Edith Tripp was one of those people. Be inspired and changed as you read the unforgettable stories of the lives of three women who were changed by the touch of the hand of almighty God. Prepare to stretch yourself to reach out and touch Him, as one woman in the Bible did, as well as these three ladies.

—Judy Jacobs
Psalmist, author

Three generations give deep perspective on healing and the pursuit of becoming more like Jesus. The miraculous battles they face and how they get through some of the greatest challenges you can encounter in life will bring His light to center stage. I encourage everyone who needs to be uplifted to read this book.

—Scott Godsey
CEO, Singing News Brands

For over forty years, Edith Tripp has been a very close, godly treasure in my life. Now may the writings of all three of these women of God continue to speak of our healing Jesus.

—Mary Y. Brown
Music That Ministers

Dedication

Mary Lou Jones was my amazing mother. I was only thirty years old when she went to heaven. She was the strongest woman I've ever known. Her faith was fierce, she was a powerful speaker, and no vision was too great for her to pursue. She was always kind, and her presence filled every room she entered. Her impact can still be felt today.

My mother and father started a missionary organization with nothing, and it's still going strong today. She was truly beautiful and strong, and her fruit will be seen in every generation. Thank you, Mom, for believing in me and helping me to understand I could do anything. This book is written in honor of the remarkable woman you were. You never stopped pressing! Thank you.

Edith Tripp: There are no words to describe this genuinely loving and beautiful woman. My dear mother passed when my husband, Robb, and I had only been married for three years. Yet in His mercy, God gave me the best gift in a "mother-in-love." That is what Edith was to me, and my mother knew I'd be okay for her to leave me safely in Edith's loving care. So, it was okay for my mother to go on to heaven at that time. I am forever grateful for the love and guidance Edith gave me in my life. Thank you!

Foreword

She was healed. These three words immediately send me there, to Luke 8 in the Bible. In my mind's eye, I can see her. She had been there, done that. She probably weighed very little, was thin and frail, ashamed, and tired of people walking around her. After all, she was considered unclean. I would assume she was also tired, and this was most likely a last-ditch effort for her to attain her healing. She had spent all that she had. However, she was *still* hemorrhaging. What a story this is! I feel her as I think of her.

She was probably dusty, and the hygiene of the day couldn't have been good, especially with her condition. But nevertheless, she pressed onward. She was clearly feisty, persistent, and unafraid. I believe she knew— something inside her innately had it figured out—that if she could simply touch Jesus, her healing would be instant. Was it her faith? Was it her endless determination and her being in the right place at the right time? Was it solely the power of Jesus? Or was it all of the above?

What creates the environment for a person to be healed? Is every healing the same? I don't know the answers to all of these questions, but this book is a treasure as it relates to this subject.

Let's take a look at the heart of the three writers in this book. Let's delve into the legacy of their family. Let me give you the perspective from my chair. You know the public story of this family: world-class evangelism with decades of television exposure all over the globe. I could speak for hours of the accolades these people have been given.

My story is a bit different. I met Shanda Tripp through a real estate transaction. Even though we had met socially at local restaurants or services, I didn't know her. On a nice Tennessee morning about a decade ago, my cell phone rang. It was Shanda, calling to ask me about a house. She introduced herself, and of course, I knew who she was. I knew she and her husband, Robb, pastored a church in my town, and I knew their family's legacy. I had loved LaVerne and Edith since I was a young girl watching them on TBN.

I liked Shanda immediately. She had grit and could comprehend the complexity of the real estate question she had asked me. I asked if they wanted me to come and meet them in person. She was anxious for me to do so. So here's my short take on that meeting: God ordained it. He sent them my way. Like the woman who touched Jesus, I, too, needed to be healed. I wasn't hemorrhaging in my physical body, but my soul was bleeding out.

When I was thirty-seven years old, I gave myself to ministry. Everything. My philosophy was this: Go big or go home. The Lord came to me and gave me specific instructions, and I said yes. I had sacrificed all the things that we sacrifice to fulfill the "call" to follow Him. The Lord blessed me, the doors swung open, and He blessed my family beyond my dreams for them. And then, shortly after my forty-ninth birthday, it was all gone. In one swipe, my entire life was shattered: My home, my calling, and my life's work imploded with a surprise divorce. I was crushed. A few years later, I found myself drowning in bitterness, vowing never to trust anyone in ministry again, except for my kids.

I ran from my place in life, pursued a real-estate sales-and-investment career, and vowed never to look back. And I didn't—until the phone call from Shanda about five years later. When I set up the meeting with Shanda and Robb, I had no idea it would change my life forever. We discussed the business of the meeting, and it went great. I liked them. After Robb was interrupted and needed to step out, I realized I needed one more signature from him, and I went to find him to obtain the signature. He signed and then said, "Can I tell you something?" Now, remember, he didn't know me. I said, "Of course." He continued, "God wants me to tell you something, and I must." I responded with my bitterness showing. I said, "You know, I don't trust preachers." He said, "That's okay. I don't, either, most of the time." I chuckled. I really liked these people! He told me a bit of his story, and I listened. Then he said, "I am telling you prophetically, God isn't through with you. Your calling wasn't attached to anyone. It was 'your calling.' Your best is still in front of you, not behind you. I appreciate your current position and ability, but this isn't for long. You're going back to ministry."

I was stunned. No one had ever had the nerve to say that to me. However, I received it. I knew it was straight from God! Within a year, I was writing books and back on the ministry battlefield. My bleeding had stopped—the bitterness was gone. God used them to "salvage" me!

Shanda Tripp has walked through an unbelievable storm. Last December she buried her precious Robb, and she buried sweet Edith within a few weeks. Even now I don't have words to describe the thoughtfulness and consideration that Shanda has exemplified. She could have quit, but she didn't. Why didn't she? Because she knows that she, too, must "press." Someone needs to read, someone needs to hear, and someone will be healed.

And sweet Edith: My last memory of Edith—she dropped by with soup and left it on my porch when I had COVID-19 last year. Again, the legacy of living out the love of Jesus was easy for her. It's who she was. It's who Shanda is. It's who sweet Hannah is. They love enough to keep walking it out on the bad days. They know that the only way to find healing from grief is to press, to find Him, and to touch Him.

Enjoy this amazing work of love that God ordained. He knew what a treasure it would be to all of us in this season.

—Kathy Crabb Hannah
Author, speaker

Preface

This book is filled with three generations of women's stories of trials, tribulations, and journeys and how they overcame all of them with the help and love of God. Shanda, Edith, and Hannah share their inspiring personal testimonies of "pressing through" sometimes unimaginable trials and unique obstacles to be met each time with the loving hand, guidance, and miracles of God.

I am writing this book out of the desire to see every woman, at any age, healed. My wish is to help everyone find out who God is and to know that anyone can conquer the challenges they may face through Him. He has already paid the price for our ultimate healing—mind, body, and soul. However, we do have a part to play. We must be willing to receive all He has done. We will find Him and be healed in the pressing forward, in the tenacity to never give up, in our faith, and in our trust in Him as our Healer.

–Shanda Tripp

Acknowledgements

Most would probably agree I had an unusual childhood. At the time, I did not realize it was uncommon, but now, upon reflection, I realize my life was very extraordinary. My family and I were always flying to Haiti or traveling to Old Mexico. We literally hosted hundreds of mission groups during that time. A typical group, or mission team, would include anywhere from five to twenty people. We would drive multiple vehicles, along with extra cars, into Old Mexico to give them away to a pastor or a family in ministry. My parents gifted well over two hundred vehicles to pastors in Old Mexico during fifty-plus years of their mission's work.

In my family, we had a lot of crazy traditions. One was that my dad would always split us up. It would depend on who was picking up or meeting our guest mission team and driving random vehicles to "give away." Every family member would be driving a different vehicle into Old Mexico. We would cross the international border between Laredo, Texas, and Nuevo Laredo, Mexico. We crossed that border more times than I can count or remember.

Getting through customs was always challenging, and we never knew which customs officer would give us a hard time. The items we were bringing into both countries were all possible "red flags" back then. In addition to the group of Americans, we would have food, "love packs," clothes, and goods to give away. Often, we carried Bibles as well as Christian literature with us. All these items could be possibly illegal. We never knew what items would be frowned upon, so my dad's strategy was to split us all up. He would put Bibles in one vehicle, with food in another, and he might put a couple members of our tour group in a different vehicle or the next. Then a different family member would drive each car.

We never had an actual planning meeting to go over what we were doing. These were "unspoken rules" we just all knew. Each of us would drive over the bridge across the Rio Grande, go through customs on our own, and if we saw each other, we would act like we didn't know one another. That was my life and very "normal" for me. Looking back, what looks insane is to let a sixteen-year-old girl—me—drive a van by myself, loaded with illegal Bibles and various other items, into a foreign country. In addition, I only spoke very broken Spanish, and no one spoke English in the customs building. Can you imagine?

Mexican customs buildings were not air-conditioned, and they were always hot and crowded. The officers were always hostile, and each one had a large gun on their hip. They were very quick to let you know they were in power: no jokes or funny business. It was not a friendly environment.

Many times, we would be "held" until we gave them a bribe. Yet I was well trained to get our mission done, and I always had money with me. It was my job to get through customs with everything for which I had been given responsibility, be it the lives of our mission team, the Bibles, or the food. This was all for the Gospel's sake.

Each time, instinctively, I pushed back any fear. I kept my head on straight, and I didn't let thoughts of danger control my mind. I would boldly proceed with confidence and get the assigned task completed. While going through customs and getting our visas, we would not see each other most of the time. We had to get all our luggage approved. Then the final task, and usually the biggest hurdle, was getting the visa for the vehicle. After we got through customs, we all knew to meet at a certain spot. It was a place past customs, past all the tourist areas. When we actually crossed the border into the interior of Mexico, there was our spot, just inside the gate.

The assignment was to get through customs and then go to the meeting spot right inside the gate. We always waited there until everyone had made it. We didn't have cell phones at that time, and no one left until everybody was together again. Sometimes we would have to wait for hours because someone might have gotten held up. It might have been caused by suspicion about the Bibles or possibly the van we were transporting to give away to a pastor. If too much time passed, we knew to start praying and send angels to help until everybody made it to the rendezvous point.

Without fail, every car, Bible, and "love pack" eventually got through. God always made a way, and the angels of the Lord were always with us. We had many scares and close calls. My father was once held in a holding cell, and some of the fellow ministers with him got down on their knees and began praying. The Mexican police finally let him go. We always wondered if it was due to God's power, or perhaps they thought my father and the others with him were crazy? It was a risk every time, but we always made it and ended up together inside the gate. We would forge ahead for the planned adventure that lay before us. The look on my dad's face would always be so happy, joyful, and full of the best kind of family pride. He would say, "You're a chip off the old block," when another family member or I would get the vehicle and the items for the Mexican people through customs. It was always his proudest moment, for which he'd trained and raised us up well. We were his good, little missionaries.

Fast-forward to my life now. I never dreamed where I would be or what my life would look like in this season. I first want to acknowledge and thank my parents, Dr. Don and Mary Lou Jones, for raising me the way they did. In the craziest way, it was instilled in me to make sure I get everything I am responsible for "all the way through the gate." I couldn't quit, allow myself to feel alone, or abandoned. I had to keep going until I got everything and everyone for which I was accountable successfully to our destination.

I have always had a deep drive to forge ahead until I got to the other side. Even though I'm by myself now, without the love of my life, I continue to press forward. It takes me back to when I was sixteen and given the adult responsibility of leading our group into the unknown.

As I look ahead, I know that I am still a part of a big family, and they're all waiting just inside the gate for me. In my childhood, it was Old Mexico, but now that gate is the gate into heaven. Thank you, Dad and Mom. I know I will make it and that you are waiting just inside the gate. I am forever grateful for my childhood and how I was trained to serve the Lord, keep the call, stick to the priority, and never give up.

To my husband of twenty-one years, Robb Tripp, the love of my life: Thank you for loving me in the most perfect way. You are the one who always encouraged me to write this book. Thank you for inspiring me and being my forever biggest cheerleader. From the first day until the last, you were my support system and my faith partner. In my heart, I know you are still cheering for me. I believe you are now with my parents and your precious mother, Edith. All of you are waiting for me, just inside the gate.

To my children, Lawson and Hannah, you both are the greatest gifts your incredible father gave me. The strength and grace from God in which I see you walking amazes me each day. Your callings will take you much further and greater than what your dad and I have done for Jesus. I am thrilled to get a front-row seat to witness the great things He has in store for both of you. You each have a world-changing call and mantle on your life.

Thank you, Mary Jackson, for encouraging me to dare to be an author. Your knowledge and inspiration have been second to none. Thank you for helping me birth this vision of a book with excellence.

Jonny and Crystal Brown and Duncan and Christie Mullins, thank you for sticking with my children and me like glue. To Jonny and Duncan, you are my husband's best friends, but I don't think he really knew how loyal and just how faithful of friends you both would be. Not only are you helping our family continue the legacy of Robb's music because you are two brilliant, world-class musicians, but you are also devoted forever friends; I thank you. Crystal and Christie, you are amazing ladies. You never left me alone, you've been willing to take on any task, you are always encouraging; I thank you for living your lives with us. I love you dearly.

Pastor Jana Hinson, thank you for your strength of character and love to our family. Thank you for leading the way with great dignity an unwavering trust in God.

To the eldership, pastors, and the church family of The Fire Place Fellowship—thank you for standing in the face of the worst of circumstances and never giving up. You have kept the faith and never left us. You have officially become my tribe to help me raise my children. Thank you. There is victory ahead.

Steve and Kathy Hannah, thank you for sharing life with us. It has truly been great. Through real estate, holidays, ministry events, and tears, you have been there for it all. Friendship, backbone, strength, courage, and advice...you are always so generous and kind to share these things with me. Thank you for running in when the rest of the world runs out.

Pastors Kent and Candy Christmas, thank you. You have been a source of strength and bold faith in the face of death. Only God knows all you have done for us. Thank you for being pastors who still do "home visits" when no one is watching. Your love and friendship have been unmatched. My children and I will never forget. Thank you. I pray for greater days ahead for all of us.

Dr. James and Lori Payne, thank you for your love and friendship with Robb and me all these years. Thank you for being a source of encouragement and for seeing in me what I could not see in myself.

Tim and Brenda Menzies, thank you for deciding to lock arms with us and not leave or get weary. Tim, you were my husband's favorite artist; this says a lot because Robb was also a very talented artist. Oh my...Robb would be amazed and thrilled to know that Tim and Brenda are so much more than artists... You are faith warriors. Thank you.

Thank you to the Tripp family for loving me as your own. What an honor to a be a part of the Tripp legacy. I love you always.

Thank you to the body of Christ. I have been amazed by the love and generosity of the saints who have helped our family. To the man who was a stranger and paid for my son's gas at the pump because you recognized him and knew his father had just died, thank you. To the unknown people who sent us meals in the hospital or food to our home, thank you. For the countless inbox messages, texts, and calls filled with words of encouragement, thank you. I have a new appreciation for the body of Christ across the board—Methodist, Presbyterian, Pentecostal, Baptist—when they all came together to show their love and support of our family. Amazing!

No other entity on the planet will pray for, care for, reach out to, and financially support its own like the body of Christ. My children and I have been reapers of the harvest of seeds sown by the generations before my precious husband, and we have reaped the benefit. Thank you for loving us. You have been the true expression of the tangible love of God on this earth. Thank you. I am so honored to be called a member of this most powerful entity. In case you need to be reminded, the body of Christ is alive, well, and fully functioning among us today.

Contents

Introduction

After years of entertaining the idea of writing a book, I finally decided it was time. I always passed on the thought before, knowing the world is full of excellent books. What could I possibly add to the literary world? At the same time, as I observed so many hurting people, my heart yearned to help.

I was raised on the foreign mission field, and mission work is one of my passions. I married my dearest Robb Tripp in 2000, and immediately we went into full-time ministry together. We had both served in ministry with our families but now it was our turn. From childhood missionary work to pastoring for decades, we have seen hurting people who need Jesus, solutions, and answers. The ultimate answer is Jesus. The breakdown for most people comes with not being able to see how the help of Jesus manifests in different ways in their lives.

I jokingly say, "When you work in ministry, people expect you to face their difficult reality with them and then go back to their river of 'denial' again alongside them." One day people will come to you crying in the depths of despair because they are hurting badly enough to get honest about their marriage, health, or children. They will share the very intimate details of their lives or their children's activities that will shock you. Then a little time goes by, things get mildly better in their situations, and they expect you to act like they never mentioned a negative word about anything. What was once a desperate prayer request has become a faint memory they do not want you to remind them of. They are no longer hurting as badly, and they have now pulled down what I like to call the "heavenly shade" on their desperate situation. They lie to themselves again and go back into their fantasy of a "perfect, social-media, covering-everything-up kind of life," pretending everything is perfect and somehow things will magically change. The fun part is that they expect you to participate in their "fantasy."

It is much easier to pretend or, as I previously mentioned, go back down the ol' familiar "river of denial." The reality of their life is often so horrible to them that they cannot bear to look at it. What they had imagined their life would be, and what their life now is, are two very different things. They don't have the strength to face themselves although they rarely want to admit it. Facing the facts of their lives would mean having to act upon that information. They might have to do something, read something, believe something, or say something, and then they might have to change. They might have to "press" forward toward what they truly want in this life.

Let's go back to the woman with the issue of blood in Luke 8. She Was Healed is a book based on her story, the story of a nameless, faceless woman who knew her truth and never gave up. If you are reading this today, are you allowing yourself to really "hear" what the Spirit is saying? You must hear the Word and then act upon it. The woman in Luke began to tell herself she needed healing. She acknowledged and spoke her truth about this. She was desperate enough that what others thought about her no longer mattered. She was determined to be healed. She was tired of people stealing from her or being told this was all her life would be. No! She wanted something different. She got honest and spoke the truth over and over again to herself. She was motivated to continue to press in, to put action behind her thoughts and to physically press in to Jesus. She pressed in with every fiber of her being. She pressed through every obstacle that came her way, every fear, other people's opinion, the fear of being denied or stopped. In truth, she pressed until she received her clearly defined, desired result: *healing.*

If you are dreaming of going for the gold in life.... not just settle, but really see the best and obtain all God has waiting for you with your name on it…if you want to overcome your struggles or your present life situation, then you are why I wrote this book. Amazingly, my wonderful, world-famous mother-in-love, Edith Tripp, and my precious daughter, Hannah Tripp, agreed to contribute to this book, as well. The three of us have a desire to see you be healed. We "got honest," hoping you will feel the encouragement and strength to do the same.

You can have family, fame, riches, or anything else you can name, but what do you really have if you are not healed, body, soul, and spirit? If a part of you or your life is broken, true abundance will never happen. You are running the race of life with a broken heel. You feel the pain that no one can see with every step, but you endure with every mile.

If any of these scenarios strikes a chord within your heart, this book is for you. The good news is that there is hope. There is a way out—a good way out. God does have "an expected end" for you (Jeremiah 29:11 KJV) that is blessed! Are you ready? Are you willing? There is a process. There is a pressing in to which you must be willing to submit your will and your life. But oh my, the joy that is soon to come! I pray you will feel the power of God touching your life with the turn of every page. I pray there is excitement in your heart. If you will take this journey with us, this book has been written to speak to your heart and give you practical life application Healing Actions with each chapter. I invite you to get off the boat floating on the "river of denial" and come on over to "Realville" with us. Join our tribe on the other side of the pain. Then you will celebrate the same testimony of your personal story ending just like this book, *She Was Healed*.

Prologue

I will never forget weeping as I kissed my children good-bye. I questioned whether I should leave my family to go "save the world." My babies were just eighteen months and four years old, and I was feeling torn between motherhood and my spiritual calling. Then my mind would return to the memories of how I was raised—to always put Jesus first and His will would be done in my life. My prayer had always been, *Whatever You ask me to do, Lord, I will do.* However, this did not relieve the heaviness in my heart. I now believe the feeling I couldn't shake was not due to the trip I was about to take, but to the assignment of death over my life. I had no idea at the time that in just a few short days I would be facing my own death.

SHE WAS HEALED

SHANDA TRIPP

CHAPTER 1

The Weapon of Praise

O LORD my God, I cried to you for help, and you restored my health. You brought me up from the grave, O LORD. You kept me from falling into the pit of death. Sing to the LORD, all you godly ones! Praise his holy name.

—Psalm 30:2–4 NLT

I grew up in Old Mexico and Haiti. My parents were missionaries, so I was excited to be going back to do the work that was so close to my family's heart and what was a typical day in life for me. I had not been back to those countries since my son had been born. Almost two years later, I was filled with excitement to travel and hoping for success in our goal of starting a Bible school—yet I had some hesitation. It was always hard for me to leave my precious babies behind, so I assumed my feelings were because of that. I finally told myself this would be a very short trip and that my kids would be safe with their wonderful father and grandmother. I then put my complete trust in God and headed out the door.

This was a destiny trip for me and I had a "calling." I was not only leading a group from the church my husband and I had founded in 2004 called The Fire Place Fellowship, but it was my first missions trip as a pastor. I was embarking on a new era in my life and carrying on my parents' legacy of the work they had begun so many years before. Ultimately, I was thrilled we had such great success on that trip.

I remember so clearly the morning we were to return home. One of the Haitian pastors wanted to pray over us for safe travels, and my thoughts were, *Brother, you have no idea. We don't need your prayers. We are going home to America, where it is safe and we have everything we need. We need to pray for you, for your safety, and for all you need here in your country. Once I get on that plane to the United States, I am safe and won't have any more problems. It's America, right?*

I returned home exceptionally late after that successful trip from Haiti, relieved that all had gone well. It was the morning of April 6, 2006, and I was jetlagged, but I decided to run a few errands for items I knew my family needed. Still exhausted, I sleepily grabbed my four-year-old daughter, Hannah, and put her in the car.

It was a dark and rainy Friday, and I had not paid any attention to the weather. My husband, Robb, said, "Do you think you should be going out in this? The weather looks pretty bad." I left anyway, thinking we'd be fine. *If I can survive Haiti, I can survive stormy weather in Gallatin, Tennessee,* I told myself. As I got in our van and began driving, I noticed the clouds looked menacing, so I turned on the radio.

Over the radio, sirens were blaring, and an announcer declared, "If you are in Gallatin, Tennessee, take cover immediately."

I looked up and saw a funnel cloud coming right in my direction. I was too far away from home, and there was no time to turn around. I panicked and went into fight-or-flight mode. I took the first left into a neighborhood and pulled into the closest driveway I saw. Their garage door was open, and a truck was parked inside. These people were complete strangers to me, but I was desperate to save my daughter and myself.

My mind raced as I scrambled out of the van and grabbed my daughter out of her car seat. The wind almost pulled her out of my arms. I remember seeing her legs go up in the air, so I ran toward the front door of the house holding Hannah as tight as I could. I started pounding on the door, screaming for someone to let us in. No one answered.

Desperate to save us both, I quickly put Hannah under the bed of the truck in the garage and climbed underneath the vehicle with her, but the wind was too powerful and I could feel it pulling at us. I looked around to see a red workbench against the back wall. I grabbed Hannah and placed her under the bench, then surrounded her with my body, both of us in the fetal position, to protect her.

Suddenly, there was a loud pop, and the hard wind stopped. Then there was no sound whatsoever. A heavy weight landed on top of me. At first, I thought maybe the workbench had collapsed on top of my daughter and me, because I could not move. Immediately I started yelling for help, hoping someone would hear me and rescue us. It was forty-five minutes later, I heard a man's voice say, "Ma'am, are you alive?"

I replied, "Yes! My daughter and I are trapped under a workbench. Can you please help us?"

He replied, "I am very sorry, ma'am, but you are underneath a collapsed brick house with a telephone pole on top of you, with live wires and gas spewing everywhere. We can't come near you. You are going to have to wait until we can get some help!"

At that moment, I remember thinking that my world had ended. The next thoughts I had were about the 9/11 victims and how they must have felt being trapped under a crushed building. And then I remembered—oh my God, the Haitian pastor had tried to pray over my safety. God had placed it on his heart to pray over us, but I was arrogant and didn't think I needed his prayers. I thought I was safe.

I was brought back from my thoughts by my daughter crying, "Mommy, I can't feel my legs," she wailed. I couldn't believe any of this was happening. But then, in a heightened state of awareness, I decided right then that my daughter and I would live! I completely focused on our survival. I made Hannah stop crying and start singing. I thought about Paul and Silas in prison, and now, while under a brick house with a death sentence now upon us, Hannah and I began to sing "We Worship You. Hallelujah."

I had no idea how much time passed. Every few minutes, someone would come and ask me, "Ma'am, are you still with us?" I would reply, "Yes," and then, after what seemed like an eternity, the ordeal ended with my good Samaritan arriving and lifting the house with a car jack. A block was placed by my head, so my skull would not be crushed if the house shifted. My good Samaritan then climbed under the house all the way to his knees. He pulled Hannah out first, then me. He laid her on a piece of siding left in the path of the storm. She was in bad shape, traumatized and in shock. She could not move her legs. I could hear her little, high-pitched voice crying for me, yet I knew she was trying to be brave. I had to trust that the men helping me and my baby girl would keep her safe for me.

These memories in my mind are as fresh as they were yesterday. It seemed like forever before my good Samaritan placed his face so close to mine and said, "Hang on... We are getting you out of here." I had no idea at that moment that his face was the last thing I would see.

Healing Actions

1. Imagine yourself completely healed, with the end pictured in your mind. Do this daily or as often as you think of it.
2. What does it look like? What does it feel like?
3. Write down as many details about your healing as you can.
4. Narrow this down to specific details.
5. Find a picture from a magazine or online that reflects these details and place it where you can see it every day.

CHAPTER 2

Because of Who He Is

Oh, the joys of those who are kind to the poor! The LORD rescues them when they are in trouble. The LORD protects them and keeps them alive. He gives them prosperity in the land and rescues them from their enemies. The LORD nurses them when they are sick and restores them to health.

—Psalm 41:1–3 NLT

By this time a group of men had been working hard to unbury me. The last few tugs on my body were the worst. Two men were trying so hard to get me out of the rubble. They kept apologizing for any pain they might be causing and assured me they were doing their best.

I remember repeatedly saying, "My name is Pastor Shanda Tripp. I am the pastor of The Fire Place Fellowship. You do whatever you need to do to get me out of here, and God will heal me." I was like a crazy woman at this point, and it was all I could say again and again.

I have reflected on this scenario many times. I believe this was my "spirit man" decreeing what I'd been pouring into my spirit for years. God was my Healer, and I could get through anything with Him. Although I was shocked and disoriented, I knew that my "spirit man" was strong, and I told the devil, angels, the men helping me, and whoever else was listening that I knew my Redeemer. Even though I was in a life-and-death situation, I knew God would heal my daughter and me no matter what.

Let me pause for a moment here to encourage you. My story is an excellent example of why the things we put in our spirit are so important. What makes all the difference in times of trial or in a life-or-death situation is what you truly believe and knowing who you are. All this must be put in your heart long before any horrible circumstance takes place. I am grateful I have spent years of my life reading God's Word, hiding it in my heart, and knowing that Jesus is my Healer. I fully believe that if I had not been diligent to read God's Word and believe the Word that I was reading, my daughter and I would have become statistics of tornado fatalities.

I believe that we are like a teabag—our true flavor comes out when we are in hot water. The difficult seasons of life prove who we really are and what we truly believe.

I remember fresh air hitting my face as my rescuers stood me up to check and see how injured I might be. I was barefoot and could feel the wet grass under my feet. My shoes had been left behind in the crushed pile of bricks where I had lain with my daughter for safety. It was still dark, windy, and gloomy outside. I opened my eyes to find Hannah, but I could only hear her, not see her. I thought maybe the dust and rubble were thick in my eyes, and I struggled to see. I didn't know if it was really dark outside or if my eyes were just covered with debris. I could see faintly out of my peripheral vision, but I was so disoriented I was not sure what was going on.

Then I felt a man come near and whisper in my ear. "I've got to get you out of here. The news is saying the tornado is turning back toward us. There are lots of trees in the road, and the ambulance can't get back here to pick you up, so I am going to take you to the hospital in my truck."

The next thing I knew I was lying across two seats in the front of a pickup truck. Someone had placed my daughter in my lap and I was so grateful to hold her. I couldn't see anything by this time, and I thought that my lungs had collapsed because I could barely breathe. But I kept praying loudly. Hannah was so upset and I told her, "Keep singing, baby, keep singing." The man driving the truck had asked me to pray for his little girl who was in kindergarten. He'd heard that the tornado had hit her school, and he hadn't received any information about whether she was okay. I began praying that God would take care of this man's little girl the way He had taken care of mine.

The ride was rough, and it felt like we were driving through the mountains, but we finally arrived at the hospital, and they rushed me in and laid me on a stretcher. By this time, I was completely blind. I begged the hospital staff to please put my daughter near me. The hospital seemed like it was in complete pandemonium, and I could sense the terror all around us. I was grateful for the care we received at a time unlike any other in my life before. The electricity was out, and the staff had to hand-pump life support to keep people alive. I kept hearing people yell, "CODE BLUE" and "STAT" all around me. Lives were lost that day, and many people were harmed or left permanently injured. This day would be remembered as one of the worst tornadoes in our city's history. I never imagined my daughter and I would need to be saved from such a tragedy.

During all this chaos and confusion, every time a medical person would leave us, I told Hannah, "Come on, girl, keep singing." There were two reasons I asked her to do this. I knew that praising God was the only way we would make it through this, and I also needed to hear my baby girl's voice because I could not see her. After what seemed like an eternity, someone finally came and spoke into my ear, "Mr. Tripp is here." I didn't know if it was my husband or my father-in-law, but I cannot express how relieved I felt that someone finally knew where we were and that we were alive.

Then I heard my daughter cry out, "Daddy!" I could not see him, but I could hear his voice and feel his familiar face close to mine. Words could not express the depth of comfort I felt that my husband was there, but I had to know where my baby boy, Lawson, was. I asked, "Is he okay?" My husband replied, "Yes, we are okay." At that moment, nothing else mattered. I suddenly had hope. Everything was going to be alright.

Hannah's hips had been crushed under the house, but God miraculously healed her. I had two broken ribs and the marrow from my bones had been released into my bloodstream. As a result, I was left blind. The eye specialist in Nashville gave me no hope that I would ever see again. I was left disabled and completely blind. Devastated is not a word good enough to describe how I felt. I could no longer cook, drive, take care of my children, or read my Bible. I realized how vital so many things were and everything I had taken for granted. Would I ever be able to read my Bible again or look into the eyes of my children or husband? Only God knew these answers.

During that time, precious church members would come to our house and help any way they could with meals and cleaning. A friend, who had been on the trip to Haiti with me, brought me a gift. On a simple sheet of lined notebook paper, she wrote out Psalm 41:1–3: *"Oh, the joys of those who are kind to the poor! The LORD rescues them when they are in trouble. The LORD protects them and keeps them alive. He gives them prosperity in the land and rescues them from their enemies. The LORD nurses them when they are sick and restores them to health"* (NLT).

My sweet husband taped the meagerly written Scripture on our headboard above where I slept. What once seemed like a lovely Scripture reading from a missionary now had become the promise from God on which I was standing. It was my only hope. I could no longer read my Bible, so I would lie on the sofa or in bed and listen to God's Word, praise music, or Christian television. This was my "new normal." It's not what I asked for, but it was where I found myself.

For countless hours, I would pray and meditate on God's Word, believing that He was my Healer. Christian television had become my new friend, and I developed a true thankfulness for it. Never had I been so dependent on anyone; now I was completely dependent on everyone—and Christian television. My sweet pastor husband would lay his hands on my eyes and pray for my sight to be restored every morning and night. I would go to sleep thinking about James 5:16: *"Therefore confess your sins to each other and pray for each other so that you may* be healed. *The prayer of a righteous person is powerful and effective"* (NIV). I kept believing that when I woke up the following day, I would see—but day after day, there was nothing. Fear and depression were constantly knocking on my heart's door, conspiring me to give up.

Six weeks went by with no change. I was hanging on to hope, clinging to my beliefs, and watching Christian TV. Someone on camera asked for anyone needing a miracle to simply believe—and that was me. *I NEEDED A MIRACLE!* As I was lying there under the Scripture that I couldn't see but that I hung on to, I began to sing a popular song. Thinking about my situation, I was having a hard time not feeling sorry for myself. Still, I forced myself to keep singing; "I Worship You Because of Who You Are..."

I started to examine my reasons for worship and praise. I was fully convinced that our praise had kept Hannah and me alive under that rubble. Yet, weeks later, here I lay, still with no sight. *Why me? Why had my faith worked to keep me alive, but it wasn't good enough or strong enough to heal me completely?* My thoughts continued... *Out of all the "bad" people in the world, I am the one with no sight.*

It's so easy for us to give up hope and feel sorry for ourselves when we are in a difficult situation. I continued to sing my way through my doubting thoughts, and then I would go back to examining my reasons for worship. Did I look at God like Santa Claus? Was I asking Him to give me what I wanted when I wanted it? Or did I really praise Him because of Who He is—my Savior, and my Redeemer?

The next thing that happened was truly life changing. There, in my bed, I made a life decision, a commitment. No matter what happened, even if I could not see anything or anyone that I loved ever again—including my husband's beautiful blue eyes, my children running and playing in the green grass at home, the breathtaking sight of the glorious sunshine bursting forth in the sky—here was my commitment: *Lord, I worship You because of who You are. You are my God and Savior...and that is enough reason to praise You.*

Soon my sight began to return. Very slowly, I recovered. I believe that once I got my "eyes" truly on Jesus and away from "woe is me," I was healed. My eyesight returned to 20/20 vision. God had given me a miracle, and my eye specialist was in complete disbelief. I had joined the ranks of those mentioned in the Bible. Just like the woman in Luke 8:47, who had the issue of blood, kept pressing through the crowd and did not get bitter at God when at first, she wasn't healed, I also took my eyes off myself. She was focused on who He was. She believed with all she had. He was the Healer, and she didn't give up. She was healed! Now that "she" was me.

Healing Actions

1. Listen to God's Word, inspiring music, and inspiring messages. Find healthy, supportive outlets.

2. Start every day by putting positive, helpful, and uplifting information in your mind and filling your internal bucket with positive, supportive words.

3. Evaluate where you are focused in life. In what direction are you headed? Decide and write it down.

4. Decide that you will not be stopped. Write about what that means to you.

5. Focus on these answers each day. Discipline yourself. Start small and change them as you change and grow.

6. Be patient with yourself.

CHAPTER 3

When She Did Not Fear

Though a thousand fall at your side, though ten thousand are dying around you, these evils will not touch you.

—Psalm 91:7 NLT

I had survived the worst event of my life. I was victorious, and I was a miracle. My eyes were completely restored, but I was still handicapped. I was broken on the inside, and I still had work to do. Fear and anxiety had set in, and I was living in emotional and mental torment every day. It felt like the enemy was waging war in my mind. My emotions and thoughts would go from one extreme to the other. I was so happy to be alive and healed, yet I was fearful of living.

I was physically healthy, but I still had a daunting task ahead of me. The day had finally arrived. It was time for me to get behind the wheel of a car and drive. The minivan I had been driving the day of the tornado ended up 900 feet away from where they pulled me out from under the house; it was as twisted as a metal can on top of the heap of rubble. Not only was my vehicle destroyed, but I now had to face my fear of driving. I had gotten a rental car, but I had refused to drive it for weeks. What once had been something so normal to do that I never used to think twice about it was now terrifying to even think about trying.

Eventually, I was able to do what I thought was an impossible thing and faced my fear head-on. I drove my car during the day, and then I drove at night. The catch was that anytime the wind blew or there was rain, I simply could not drive. I would stand for hours and watch the cloud progressions. I listened to the weather constantly and learned about the different kinds of clouds and how they traveled. I became a self-taught meteorologist. I never saw a therapist, but I am sure I was suffering from PTSD.

My fears went beyond driving. Every time my children were in the bathtub, I had a horrible fear that if I looked away, even for one minute, when I turned back around, they would have drowned. When my son was in the highchair, I would imagine he was choking. Sometimes when I was driving, I would have wild visions of being in a terrible car wreck. Whether in a restaurant, church, or a shopping center, my first thought was always, *If a tornado hits, where will I hide?* I would instantly find, in my mind, the safest place or have a plan ready for what to do in case of an emergency. Day in, day out, this was my torturous life.

One night I was a guest speaker at a women's event in South Carolina. We were in a high-rise hotel when a horrible storm came in, and I could feel the building sway. I was a basket case, ready to climb under the chairs, but we were in a ballroom, and there was no place for me to take cover. The fear and constant reliving of the trauma my daughter and I had gone through was nagging, relentless, and always with me. I would dream about the tornado when I slept. I would wake up asking myself what I could have done differently. Was I a horrible mother for driving into the storm that day? Why did I allow myself to get into such a horrific situation? If I had made such a stupid decision once, what if I did it again? I repeatedly replayed that day's events in my mind, hour after hour, hoping for a different ending.

Anytime it would rain when I was at home, I would be ready to put my children and myself into a tiny closet. I was constantly prepared for the worst. I could see the toll this was taking on my husband and family. Guilt set in for what this was doing to them. I was acting like a crazy woman. If the wind blew hard at all, I completely shut down emotionally. Family and friends would call to see if I was okay if they knew rain or a storm was coming. Everyone knew my emotional and mental state had been traumatically altered. A few times, when my husband Robb could not be home and there was a thunderstorm, our church staff or friends would sit with me until it was over. My life was surreal. It was a never-ending nightmare, constantly playing on a screen in my mind.

One specific day I was driving the car with both of my kids in the back seat. Fear and torment were along for the ride, as well. I came to a two-way stop and was about to turn across traffic. In came all of the fearful thoughts flooding my mind: *If you don't turn this car correctly, the oncoming traffic will hit this vehicle and kill your children. You better be careful, or everything you love will be gone.* It was like a tidal wave filling my head with every wicked thought possible. Then I spoke those two little words that changed everything in my mind: *"JESUS, HELP!"* Suddenly, like a flood, I felt the Spirit of God come into the car, calm me, and enter my mind.

As the evil thoughts tried to come in, I felt God's Spirit ask me these questions: *What if you finally know who you are in Christ, and what if you realize I have already given you all the power you need over this evil? What if you finally take your authority and rightful place to have peace of mind? What if you put on the helmet of salvation and receive the peace I have already paid for you? What if you finally realize who you are in Christ and that the devil has already been defeated?*

I then began to use this same weapon, against the devil, that had saved my daughter and me from under the rubble: my praise! I started praising God in my car right then, and revelational knowledge filled my spirit. I had been allowing the enemy to control my mind with fear. This all-consuming fear had only happened because I had not kept Jesus on the throne in my mind. I had not been walking in the authority God had given me over the enemy.

I love this verse: *"Let not your heart be troubled"* (John 14:27 NKJV). I feel we often miss these most important words. This has been a very important verse to me, and I am brought back to it from time to time.

I finished my errands, and as soon as I arrived home and got my children settled, I sat down and reached for my Bible. It fell open to an oh, so familiar passage, this verse from Psalm 91: *"A thousand may fall at your side, and ten thousand at your right hand, but it shall not come near you"* (ESV). I heard it say that if a tornado happens near you, though the house on your left collapses or the house on your right falls apart, it shall not come near your home. At that moment, I felt a surgeon's scalpel come into my heart and stomach and remove the fear. I sat there and just kept reading that Scripture repeatedly, and as I did, I could feel the burden of fear I had been carrying around release its grip from my spirit. It may sound crazy, but that day at my kitchen table, I was set free of the spirit of fear from the traumatic experience of the tornado.

I had not just been physically damaged, but I was emotionally damaged as well. I needed the hand of God to touch my life. I believe many people have also suffered a significant loss in their lives and may have come through and healed physically. However, emotionally they are still profoundly broken and wounded. They have not yet allowed the Holy Spirit to heal them.

I have seen people in wheelchairs or on crutches be quickly helped, assisted, or prayed over by the elders at church. Their wounds were there for everyone to see. I felt just as broken and needing help, but no one could visibly see my wounds or pain to reach for me and help. I needed the touch and support that only God could give. I was like the woman who bled, knowing that touching Jesus would bring complete healing. I had to get out of myself and the fear that was controlling me, then surrender that fear completely to God. All my knowledge, teaching, learning, and beliefs finally came to my rescue. I have witnessed God's great power at work in me throughout my life, and it guides me still.

We must get into God's Word to change our thought process. Changing the way we think takes time. You can decide to do it, but you must be willing to do the work to make it your truth. It takes speaking and declaring what God says about you and what He says about your family. In Scripture, an angel or Jesus would say, "Fear not, only believe." Fear is ordinary and usually the first response people have to frightening and traumatic situations. Still, it takes an intentional effort of putting God's Word continually in your heart for faith to become your automatic response when the enemy of fear comes knocking on your mind's door. I was healed from fear and anxiety because I let God have His way in my heart, and He continues to change the way I think. No fear—no more!

I fully believe that many women are broken in our society today. Statistically, one in eight women deals with depression in America. We are the wealthiest nation, yet we are the most drugged up. How can that be with all the resources and freedom we have? More pharmaceutical pills are distributed for depression, anxiety, and insomnia, and Americans buy much more medicine per person than any other country in the world.

It is a scientific fact that fear, especially experienced early in life, is directly linked to mental disabilities later in life. With low self-esteem or no sense of self-value, many people have been conditioned to believe they are not worth anything or worth being loved. That is a lie that produces fear and insecurity. This sometimes leads people to self-medicate so they can numb how they feel. Rather than facing the fear that has crept into their hearts and dealing with it, they accept it as their sentence in life. They think this is the way they are supposed to live, and the lie they believe is a garden to manage, not an evil root they need to rip up and throw away.

Healing Actions

1. Think about what you really believe and "know." Write it down and analyze it.
2. It's time to get emotionally honest with yourself about yourself. Be willing to look at the good and the bad in your life so that you can heal. Don't hesitate to get help if needed.
3. Once you know your actual situation, you can evaluate your next best plan of action.
4. Are you emotionally wounded and need help?
5. Is it physical healing you desire, or do you need healing for both?

CHAPTER 4

Facing the Truth

The LORD is close to all who call on him, yes, to all who call on him in truth.

—Psalm 145:18 NLT

In 2004 my husband and I founded The Fire Place Fellowship, in Hendersonville, Tennessee. We were young, ambitious, and very eager. A few weeks after our first service on a Sunday morning, I was in our only, tiny office. A few minutes before the next service was supposed to start, an usher spoke to me and said that there was a woman who wanted to meet with me before the service began. I instantly said, "Of course, send her back." The usher replied, "Well, you need to know, her husband has severely battered her. She is in bad shape and asking for you."

I was shocked because I knew this woman and I had no idea she was in an abusive relationship. I was perplexed. How could this be, and more importantly, what could I possibly do for her? Sadly, this was the first of many encounters I would have with women over the years who were or had been abused by someone with whom they chose to be in a relationship.

One of the most profound abusive situations I can remember, which has always stuck with me and haunted my memories, was that of a church member named Laura. In 2009, she was our (Pre-K) Wee-Warrior director. She served with joy and faithfulness. We had never had a team member in the children's department who had served with such excellence.

Laura was married to a man named Bill, who attended church occasionally. Laura had been coming to our church for several years. Yet she never discussed her personal life or her marriage, and she never complained. So it was very shocking when she informed us that she and Bill were getting divorced after twenty-five years of marriage.

On a Wednesday night after church, I will never forget our conversation. A large group of us went out to eat Mexican food. Laura sat on my left, and her young adult son sat on my right. Between snacking on the baskets of chips and dip, she told me about the years of abuse she had endured. I had no idea how to help, but I assured her I would pray for her. I remember leaving the restaurant that night with a heavy heart, hoping she and Bill could somehow work things out.

Forty-eight hours later, Robb and I were going to a home fellowship group meeting on a Friday night. A young family who belonged to our church was hosting the meeting. We arrived about seven o'clock that evening. This meeting was an event that Laura always attended. As Robb and I got there, the host of the home informed us that Laura had stopped by and left a cake for us, but she could not attend that night. Our church was hosting a baby shower for Laura's grandchild the next morning, so she was out running errands and preparing for that event.

My cell phone rang about an hour into our fellowship meeting. Laura's nine-month pregnant daughter was screaming on the phone, "Please pray for me!" My first thought was that maybe there was something wrong with the baby, or perhaps she was going into labor. Oh, how I wish it had been either. The daughter was calling to tell me that her dad, Bill, had just shot her mother, Laura. She and her three-year-old daughter were hiding in the bedroom closet, hoping her dad wouldn't shoot her or her little girl next. My mind could hardly register what I heard in that moment.

I stayed on the phone with Laura's daughter while my husband, our associate pastors, and I jumped in the car and headed straight for her house. My husband drove like the house was on fire. The rest of us began praying, hoping this wasn't real, that maybe it was a false alarm or a misunderstanding. Then Laura's daughter hung up abruptly. We knew something was really wrong. Meanwhile, several people at the home meeting with us had called the police. As we got closer to the little white house in an average neighborhood, we could see the police lights flashing everywhere.

Clearly, something serious was happening. We parked our car as close as we could, then got out of the car and walked up to the house. As we approached, we could see that crime scene tape had already been placed around the scene where something had taken place. There was a large object on the ground behind Laura's car. I recognized her car because I had seen it at church so many times. The large object was in the shape of a body and was covered in a white cloth.

At that moment, I am sorry to admit, with everything in me I wanted whatever was under that white sheet to be Bill. I was hoping there had been an accident, not an intentional murder. Surely our precious Laura was not lying dead on that cold, dirt-and-gravel driveway.

The temperature was dropping. I remember leaning against a large oak tree because the police would not let us get closer to the house. My husband identified himself as the family's pastor, and the officers let him get closer. Standing at that tree, I began to shake uncontrollably. I thought it was from the cold, but the trauma of what I was watching was affecting my whole body.

What seemed like forever was suddenly interrupted by a car pulling up in the middle of the street. A young man got out of the vehicle. It was Laura's son. He had just been sitting next to me two nights before, eating chips and talking. He ran up to the barricade trying to get through, but a police officer stopped him. The next thing I saw was my husband and an officer approaching him. My husband grabbed him in a giant bear hug and held him up as the police officer informed this young man that his father had just murdered his precious mother.

I will never forget the bloodcurdling roar of a scream that came from him. I could see his breath in the cold night air. His body was convulsing with grief, and my husband just continued to hold him even tighter. Then he screamed "No, no, no!" My sweet husband would not let him go.

I remember looking at the streetlamps that were lighting the scene we had just witnessed. It was as if Laura's son's mourning cries were bouncing off the streetlamps, making an echo down what should have been a quiet, typical, small-town street. But that night, instead of these lamps lighting the way for innocent children to play and for families to gather, they were lighting the results of pure evil, tragedy, and the great sorrow that had just occurred.

Bill had come to his pregnant daughter's house, and he saw his wife, Laura, unloading sacks from the store filled with items for the baby shower. He had asked Laura if she could talk, and she said, "Yes, just let me get the rest of the bags from my car."

As Laura grabbed those last few bags from her trunk, she looked at Bill face-to-face. Bill then shot her at close range. He stood over her and unloaded the full round of eight shots into her and completely decimated her head and body.

His pregnant daughter witnessed this from inside the house at the front window. She grabbed her three-year-old daughter and called the police. She then called me, her pastor, in hiding at that point, because she truly believed Bill was coming after her and her daughter to kill them next.

As time went on, we learned the full extent of how bad the abuse had been. Laura had suffered for years. She had been conditioned since her childhood that she was not worthy of healing herself, so she never took steps to leave the abusive relationship until it was too late. Laura was never strong enough to stand up for herself and press through the crowd, like the woman in Luke 8.

There are really no words to tell you how this affected me. Laura's story forever changed my opinion of domestic abuse and how I have counseled people with any control or domestic issues. I now view relationships and someone with self-esteem issues very differently, as well. If you really dissect domestic abuse, it always comes down to "control." Many times it's very slow, and it creeps in quietly. The devil does not come to us bold and dressed in a red cape with a pitchfork. No, he usually sneaks in with very small, tiny lies, tricks, and deceptions. And then he slowly takes over your thoughts and eventually your actions until he has complete control.

Years later, while in prayer, God took me back to every woman I had ever met and counseled, even our precious Laura. God revealed to me that I was truly powerless to help them in every case if the woman did not act on her own real truth. No one can help someone who stays in an unhealthy or abusive relationship. They must choose to stop believing the lies. I personally wanted to kick every wife-abusing, controlling, and insecure spouse out of their house. It was enough! But I can't go to their house and fix their problems. They will only get free from abuse when they have had enough and are strong enough to press their way through the situation, believing they deserve better. Then they can be healed and free from the grips of abuse.

I have reflected on Laura and Bill's story, and in a small way, it is part of my story, too, because God only deals in truth for each of us. He is Truth. God can't operate in the realm of lies as we can. The Bible tells us in so many Scriptures about lies, where they will lead us, and how they cannot enter the kingdom of heaven. I have come to understand the biggest lie most people tell is to themselves. In a way, it is a betrayal of the self, if you think about it. People can come to church or attend a Bible study every day but never really get honest with God or themselves. Recovery organizations like AA have people "take inventory" of themselves and their lives. It's time for us to start doing that for ourselves so we don't end up in miserable or life-threatening situations.

Laura always seemed pleasant and never complained. I never dreamed she didn't know her worth by how she acted. I had known her for years and only found out about the abuse she had endured forty-eight hours before she died. Laura never truly saw her own value or her truth in this life. Even though she attended church, I don't think she understood who she was in Christ. It was God's will for her to be healed physically, mentally, and spiritually. But if she never knew that, or what her self-worth was in God's love, she certainly couldn't have realized she was worth being loved in a healthy way by a human man on this earth.

I was there for her, along with her church family, and we would have done anything to help her. But we, like God, can only deal in truth. We can only help according to what we are told. Suppose someone tells themselves that everything is "okay" or blindly believes that things will magically get better without counsel or God's help. In that case, they are only lying to themselves. They live in a fantasy world, but in reality, things will only get worse. Say "enough" to the abuse, the toxic cycle, the fear of failure, the physical sickness in your body, the broken relationships, the depression, and all the other detrimental effects of the abuse. Let go of the feelings of competition and that you are not enough. It's time to stop telling yourself lies. A weak spirit attracts attacks. A strong spirit will be the power plant in your life.

Healing Actions

1. To start healing from any lies you are telling yourself, you can begin by removing yourself from rooms, places, and situations in which you don't belong.

2. You must be willing to take ownership of the lies you have been telling yourself, in order to heal from them. This can be challenging, but just take it one day at a time.

3. Try to be with like-minded people who seek the same things in their lives.

4. Speak and read the Word of God each day. Carry those words in your mind and heart so they become your primary verbiage.

5. If you are in a bad relationship, especially if it is abusive, find someone to whom you can talk and determine how to get yourself out of it.

6. Read God's Word. Learn who you are in Christ. Build your inner faith man to really believe and know your identity in Christ. Then you will stop letting the devil steal from you.

7. Never pass on abuse to someone else.

8. Call the Domestic Abuse Hotline at 1-800-799-7233 if you need to.

HANNAH TRIPP

A note to my daughter, Hannah:

I remember your genuine faith, for you share the faith that first filled your grandmother Lois and your mother, Eunice. And I know that same faith continues strong in you.

— 2 Timothy 1:5 NLT

I remember your genuine faith, for you share the faith that first filled your grandmother, Edith, and Mary Lou and your mother, Shanda. And I know that same faith continues strong in you.

Robb and I were so excited the day we found out we were having a baby. When we shared the news with her grandpa, LaVerne Tripp, he immediately said, "This child will go around the world with the Gospel." Those words just came out of his spirit before I even knew what the sex of our baby would be. Three others prophesied that our child would go around the world with the Gospel. With so many powerful declarations and words of knowledge, Robb and I knew for sure that this child would be...a boy! Boy, were we wrong!

This unborn child, who had so many bold words declared over her, was the most beautiful, strong-willed, curly-haired, outgoing little girl I had ever seen, and she still is that spunky *GIRL!* I am reminded of the words of 2 Timothy 1:5. She was destined before birth with so many gifts from previous generations, and I have known that in her life, nothing will stop her or God's plan for her life.

Even with all the promises and prophecies spoken over her, both Hannah and I have still had to deal with many of the cruel realities of life. Hannah has faced a multitude of things in her life that other people's faith might not have helped them survive. But our Hannah is strong in the Lord, even though both of her amazing grandmothers are now with Jesus, and she had to say her final good-bye to her most wonderful father, Robb Tripp, at the age of twenty. You might think life has not been fair to Hannah, but we say, "None of that changes what God has planned for her." Hannah's faith, that generational faith, still stands. Hannah will do and be what God has destined for her to do and to be in this life. Her dad and I are so proud of her. This book is a step toward that destiny for her. Her dad knew it; her "Elie" grandmother knew it, and I hope she can inspire you as you read the following two chapters written by our very own world-changer, Hannah Tripp.

Your mother loves you, always,
Shanda

CHAPTER 5

The Fake Flock

by Hannah Tripp

We are hard pressed on every side, but not crushed; perplexed, but not in despair; persecuted, but not abandoned; struck down, but not destroyed.
—2 Corinthians 4:8–9 NIV

People want to get close to pastors and ministers, but not always for the right reasons. Sometimes they just want to run down their ministry and destroy the pastor's reputation.
—Hannah

When I was sixteen, my dad was having some health issues and it was a rough time for all of us. People who knew us were aware of what was happening with my dad. One day I was at the grocery store, and I saw a couple who used to attend my parents' church. I knew they were troublemakers and had been manipulative in the past, so I was not going out of my way to talk to them. I was on the snack aisle and thought they hadn't seen me, but the next thing I knew, they came up to me and started bombarding me with questions about my family. They even blocked me in so I couldn't leave.

This couple had manipulated and used my family and me in the past. I wanted to get away from them as fast as I could. When they asked how my family was doing, I told them we were very well because I didn't want them to know about my dad's health issues. The couple appeared sad to hear we were "doing well" and continued asking questions, including whether we were disappointed they had left our church. I finally answered, "No," to all of their questions and I walked away.

I thought that was the end, but they waited for me to check out and followed me out to my car, continuing to ask questions about my family, obviously to stir up trouble. I thought to myself, Now, Hannah, what are you going to do? In a moment of anger and frustration, I asked them to please stop talking to me. The couple then told me I was not acting like a good pastor's daughter and that I should be ashamed for ruining my Christian reputation. If protecting my family and refusing to give our personal information to people who have less-than-positive intentions for us is considered not being a good Christian, then so be it.

Looking back on situations like this, I see how I allowed others' deceit and toxicity to create bitterness inside of me. People, like this couple, are tests to see if I would bow to the bitterness or if I would rise above the issue that is standing right in front of my face. People like this also love to throw up the facade to others' of being close to pastors' and their families and then they turn around and bash them, leave them, and run them straight into the ground and then want pastors to act like nothing ever happened. People like this have ill intentions and unfortunately, sometimes in my life, like this instance, I didn't rise above the test. I allowed myself to become bitter against God, the church, my parents, and myself.

In another night I remember clearly, I was at an event at our church around Christmastime. There were guest speakers and singers, and it was a perfect night of worship with friends and family. At this event was a woman who used to attend our church. She had placed curses on our family with death threats—she hated us and wanted us all dead. She had come that night because she had wanted to see one of the guest speakers.

After the event, I went to the restroom without knowing this woman was following me. As I was washing my hands at the sink, she stood in front of the door, cornered me, then asked me several questions.

"Why are your parents in such good health?"

"Don't you think your parents would be better off dead?"

"You seem to be a good Christian girl, but with the kind of mother you have, you'll never make it in life. Wouldn't you agree?"

I stood there baffled by this woman who was in her late sixties. I was only eighteen. Why would she say such things to me? Now, I always want to show the love of Jesus to others, but we are never called to be door-mats to other people. I politely asked her if I could leave the restroom because I genuinely had no idea what to say to her. She then told me I could not leave until I answered her questions the way she wanted me to. I pulled out my phone and texted someone, asking them to please come get me out of there. Thankfully, the re-stroom door opened with someone coming in to rescue me, and I was able to slip away. But as I was walking out to the foyer, the same woman grabbed my arm and told me I wasn't allowed to leave until I answered her questions. Finally, an usher told her to leave me alone and it would be best if she left for the evening because she was being inappropriate. She was not happy, of course, and she stormed out of the church.

The toxicity of others like this has really affected me and helped create a wall of bitterness, which I allowed into my heart. Ultimately this led to my bitterness against the church.

Growing up in a pastors' home, I have seen and experienced many things. People come and go, and that is life, but the difference when your parents are pastors is the degree and type of involvement that comes with it. Pastors dedicate babies to Jesus, attend kindergarten graduations, pray with teens, teach young adults, marry adults, and bury the elders. They visit the jail cells of anyone who is in need, feed the homeless, and give money away where it is needed. They give their time, blood, sweat, and tears. They sacrifice their all and lay down their life. All for what?

I have sat and pondered this question: How can people act like they love you and your family, only to leave your church or any other church for reasons like the church walls weren't the right color or the music was too loud—or maybe the message being preached was too convicting, and they really didn't want to have to change their lives, or perhaps the person is more concerned with who is at church than really the reason for being at church, which is Jesus Christ? There are those who will crucify ministers quickly, but then turn around and call them asking for prayer the next day.

When people leave the church, they often expect their pastors to later accept them back like nothing ever happened. And you know what pastors with good hearts do? They take them right back and pray with them. Jesus would do this, and that's the One we are all striving to be like, right? I have often wondered why people leave a church and talk so badly about it, along with the pastors, ministers, and other members. When this happens, it breaks my heart because sometimes you become so close to these people. They become like family.

I have been blessed with the best family in the entire world, and for that I am very grateful. My grandfather, LaVerne Tripp, is a living legend; he wrote songs considered "staples of the church." My grandmother, Edith Tripp, is the most loving person on this planet, who has traveled the world, and she can cook like no other! My father is an amazing pastor and Grammy award–winning studio musician who grew up on the road. My mother is a missionary at heart who grew up in a missionary's home in Haiti and Old Mexico. She continues to carry on her parents' legacy and their missionary work of over fifty years.

My parents and family were led into this kind of work because that's what you do when God calls you to do something like ministry and mission work. I am blessed to live in a stable home where Jesus is first and ministry is our life, but that does not protect us from people who want to see our family's ministry fail. They come into our lives sometimes with ill intentions. I learned to be careful and never get too close to people because they might leave in the blink of an eye and frankly, they probably will. I've been through it numerous of times. I learned to always act like everything was okay and that I was okay, no matter what.

In doing this and not facing the reality of the truth of how situations like I shared affected me, I was struggling. These circumstances opened the door to sleepless nights when I would find myself depressed and not wanting to live—nights when I could not see past my current situation. But I finally realized I had to face what I was going through and how I felt so that I could heal. I now know that it's okay to talk about my problems and struggles because maybe my testimony can help someone else.

Healing Actions

1. Tell someone you know—perhaps an adult, a friend, or someone in your church—if you are being bullied. Don't remain silent.
2. Stay away from toxic people and those with bad behavior or ill intentions.
3. Stop and capture negative, fear-filled words or influences in your mind. Catch them and replace them with positive ones.
4. If what you are saying doesn't align with your end goal, change it.
5. Be an example to others by speaking positive words.

CHAPTER 6

Disguised Deception

by Hannah Tripp

Hope deferred makes the heart sick, but when the desire comes, it is a tree of life.
—Proverbs 13:12 NKJV

I had finally let go of toxicity, so I did my hair and makeup for the first time in over a year, just for me because I wanted to, not for anyone else. In late April 2021, my photo memories popped up on my phone, reminding me that I had been lying in my bed, crying my eyes out, just a year before because I was so heartbroken. I wanted to feel accepted, loved, and beautiful—all the things everyone my age desires. After my heart was broken, I gave up on God and decided to do my own thing.

That, of course, was the biggest mistake I ever made. Because I am a pastors' kid, it is expected by others that I automatically love church and love serving the Lord. I've always loved God and knew there was a calling on my life, but at that time, I decided to live life my own way, on my own terms, because I was so hurt and tired of church and serving the Lord.

I hear people say all the time there is no difference between the lead pastors' kids, the associate pastors' kids, the children's pastors' kids, the youth pastors' kids, but there is. Do not compare yourself, criticize, crucify, or tear down the pastor's family until you have been in their actual positions as lead pastors. It is a whole lot harder than one could even bare to think.

Growing up as a pastors' kid, I led a very normal life. I went to school, competed in sports, hung out with friends, and attended normal activities like all the other kids. At the same time, my home life was wonderful, yet being a pastors' kid made my life difficult at times. Other kids wouldn't like me as soon as they found out I was the daughter of pastors. I got left out, blocked on social media, bullied, and cyberbullied. I was manipulated by others thinking they were my friends when all they would do was tear me down or just use me in the end. In middle and high school, I would leave early during some school days because I couldn't handle the secret bullying that I was experiencing.

My "friends" were nice to me in front of everyone else, but when we were alone, I felt like my life was a constant struggle of "not being enough." I could not live up to these people's expectations, and I never would. Bullies hurt others because they are hurting themselves. It is never ever about the one being bullied. They are broken somehow and take it out on anyone who is vulnerable. Bullying also involves jealousy and wanting what others may have or thinking that they aren't as good as other people, or even good enough at all.

One of the ways I overcame the hurt and pain of bullying in person and on social media was to take a step back and realize I was not the problem; they were. I am called and chosen by God, and no one can ever take that away from me. No one can ever take that away from you, too. I still had to grow, learn, and heal. Keeping my problems and hurts a secret was not the answer. Not dealing with the pain and hurt in my life only made it come back ten times worse.

After graduating from high school, I got into a very unhealthy relationship. I didn't realize it at the time, but I was still attracting toxic people into my life and carrying around the bitterness and hurt inside me from my childhood and school years. I was manipulated by people I had thought were my friends in middle school. In high school, I was used by people close to our family. Then I found myself in a relationship where I was deceived, manipulated, used, drained, hurt, and emotionally abused. I was still attracting the same demons into my life because I was the one who was broken. I never dealt with my wounds from the painful church experiences I had gone through. It overflowed into my personal life and would have ultimately killed me if God had not intervened.

I stayed in the toxic cycle of a horrible relationship for so long because I had hoped the other person would change. Maybe if I waited long enough, I thought, they would change; if I could just be enough for them, they would change. This is an endless cycle that will never change unless you remove yourself from the unhealthy situation and get yourself healthy. We must be whole to be in a healthy relationship with someone else.

I finally got tired of the people with whom I was hanging out, tired of being hurt, and tired of crying my eyes out every night, wondering why I was not enough for others. I let the devil play with my mind for too long, and I'd had enough!

What I have learned in the past year is that the devil only brings you things that look wonderful. He will never put someone in your life or something in front of your face that looks terrifying or scary. It would not be attractive to most of us, and we would not find it pleasing to our eyes.

I went through a season of brokenness, and looking back now, it makes me laugh to even think I could live my life on my own terms. That was a prideful thought, and I repented for having this mindset for too long. I decided to put God first and then myself, ahead of toxic people, relationships, and friendships.

I realized something that I have noticed most people who have been church hurt do not seem to realize. I realized that God never hurt me, people did. Why did I give up on God when it was people who hurt me to begin with? God isn't weird, people are. God doesn't hurt you, people do. God never left me, people left me. You see, we tend to blame God for things that God was never involved in from the start and then we get upset, bitter, and hurt when people do us wrong and we blame it on God, we leave the church, and never return. I would have to say, in the midst of my bitterness, suffering, torment, and pain, I realized that God was drawing me back in because God never intended for me to step out of His Will in the first place.

Even if you haven't stepped out of the Will of God but the church has hurt you, I'm sorry about that, but join the club. We've all experienced hurt one time or another. It's time to forgive and move on. It's time to realign with God's Word, and it's time to get back into fellowship with believers in Christ and fulfill His calling for your life!

There are teachers, lawyers, and doctors who mess up every single day but yet we still attend school, hire more lawyers, and visit the doctor. When one pastor offends you, or even has a personal failure, we turn our backs on God and hate the church for the rest of our lives. Why? Did you know pastors' are still people too? If one pastor makes you give up on God and you never return to the church and His people, then clearly your priorities are out of line and I highly encourage you to observe your heart and surrender back over to the Lord, just like I had to do. I became so jaded and was done with the ministry ... BUT GOD!

I thank God today for loving me enough to draw me back in even though I got myself into a mess but that mess has now shifted my focus back to God and God has removed the hurt, the pain, the bitterness, the sin that had me bound, and He broke the blinds of jadedness off my eyes and now I am set free through the power of the Holy Spirit. I got free because I pursued it. I pressed through when I didn't feel like it. I made a decision to get healed and I got what I believed for. Just like the woman with the issue of blood, I made a decision to get what I deeply desired - which was my healing.

Doing my hair and makeup might seem like a small thing to you, but it was a big deal to me because no one was there the nights I cried myself to sleep or on the days I couldn't handle what was going on around me anymore, or when I wanted to give up. But you know what I learned? I learned that Jesus was there.

Jesus was always there, no matter how many times I ran away from Him. He was there when I was stuck in a toxic cycle of my own sin from my bad decisions. Jesus was with me when I left myself and forgot who I was meant to be. When I was caught in a relationship with a narcissist and was being gaslighted, God never left me, not one single time. I am fully convinced that the only life worth living is the life lived in the will of God. I wouldn't have it any other way.

One day after I let go of some relationships in my life that no longer were good for me, I decided to write down some confessions to retrain my brain. I wanted my ears to hear my mouth say the words. I didn't believe the words at first, and I wasn't sure if it would work. But that's why you have to keep saying it repeatedly until it becomes your truth – you have to press through and not give up.

If you are strong enough to be in an unhealthy relationship, you can find a way to get out. If you are capable of getting addicted to something negative, then you are capable of breaking that addiction, as well. Even if you don't believe it or know what to do, you can heal with the love and guidance of Jesus. If you are reading this and still breathing, you can start a healthy, new life today. Just put one foot in front of the other, moving from one moment to the next. Take a deep breath and move forward.

These are the confessions I wrote down that day. Feel free to use these for yourself.

> *Today is the day.*
> *Today is the day I walk away from all of the hurt and heartbreak I have caused myself.*
> *Today is the day I choose what is best for me.*
> *Today is the day I decide I am going to have a better life than what I have right now.*
> *Today is the day I am going to make sure that I am a whole person again.*
> *Today is the day I let go of the attachment that I have to negative things.*
> *Today is the day I am saying good-bye to the person or the thing that has caused me pain.*
> *Today is the day I give my heart back to God.*
> *Today is the day I surrender my desires, my will, my emotions, and myself back to Jesus Christ.*
> *Today is the day I choose healing over heartbreak.*
> *Today is the day I choose joy over pain.*
> *Today is the day I choose to value myself.*
> *I am a miracle in the making.*

Healing Actions

1. Make a list of your own positive confessions. Write them in your words specific to you, sharing how you feel, and what you are going through.
2. Get as detailed as you can but be specific.
3. Declare the Word of God over yourself daily.
4. Decide who you are in Christ and do not let the world tell you any different.
5. Learn to know your boundaries so you can have healthier relationships.

EDITH TRIPP

When I was around fifteen years old, TBN was on the television in the family living room, as it usually was in those days, and the Tripp family was on the screen. I had never met them or even seen them in a live concert. There was Edith, with a headband on, giant earrings, one black stocking, one red stocking, and of course, high heels. Glam to the max! I turned *to my friend who was with me in the room and said, "When I grow up, I want to be just like Edith!" I had no idea those were prophetic words. There was no way I could have known that someday, that beautiful, over-the-top lady on the screen would be my mother-in-love.*

Edith was every bit as wonderful in person as she was on the screen. Always loving. Always giving. The absolute best cook, mother, grandmother, and friend. If you knew her, you loved her. Most likely, she gave you something. She was the most giving person ever. I was blessed to have twenty-four amazing years spent with her. We spoke about this book for about three years. She recognized my daughter and her granddaughter, Hannah, as having a gift for writing. Edith had been asked to write a book many times, yet she always declined. But this time, we got a yes, as long as ultimately it gave Hannah a boost in the writing world. We finished the book in the fall of 2021. Before we would get the first printing, Edith went to be with Jesus. This book is the last gift she left for all of us. Thank you, Edith Tripp. The world is truly a better place because you were in it. Thank you for showing us how to walk in love and how we can be truly healed.

I love you always,
Your daughter-in-love,
Shanda Tripp

CHAPTER 7

No One Ever Cared For Me Like Jesus

by Edith Tripp

Cast all your anxiety on him because he cares for you.

—1 Peter 5:7 NIV

BORN DEAD IN A RED HOUSE
—I give my praise to Him.—

My sisters and I call it the "Big Red House." It was the place where my mom gave birth to me. It was a four-room house, and back when I was born, lots of moms had their babies at home. In the back bedroom is where my mother's labor began. After thirty-six hours of horrendous labor, the doctor looked at my dad and grandmother and said, "I can save either your wife or your baby."

My dad said, "Save my wife."

I came into this world already dead. The doctor wrapped me in a blanket and laid me at the foot of the bed, then he proceeded to save my mother's life. My grandma said the Spirit of the Lord came over her, and she began to pray. She laid her hands on my lifeless little body as I was bundled up in a blanket, and she rebuked death. She reminded God of His words: *She will live and not die, but declare the works of the Lord.* (Psalm 118:7.)

My grandma used God's authority to declare that her *seed will touch nations.* She then unwrapped the blanket and said she felt movement come into my body. I let out one scream and then a cry. The enemy thought he had won, but God won. Praise God for the Holy Spirit that filled my grandmother that day. *So I pour my praise on Him.*

When I was about nine years old, my mother had just had her fifth daughter, and she was in bed with her in the same room where I was. It was cold, so my mother asked me if I could put some coal in the heater. I wanted to be smart and make the fire blaze even hotter, so I poured gasoline on it, and when I did, the fire jumped out on me. My hair, face, and hands were on fire. My mom jumped out of bed, threw a blanket over me, picked me up, took me to the kitchen, and put cold water on me. I lost my hair, and there were blisters all over my skin, face, and hands. I had third-degree burns. My mom and dad began to pray and confess that I would not be disfigured or scarred. Within a week, I woke up and had no scarring or disfigurement! *I give praise to Him.*

My mother and daddy separated when I was eleven. She met another man and got involved with him while working as a waitress in a restaurant. She never really loved my daddy and had married him only to get away from her home.

One night I remember sitting in the bathroom while my mom was in the bathtub, and she told me she was gonna go away, but that she would come back for my sisters and me. My mother did not return for five long years. It was an incredibly painful time for all of us. Even though we were all devastated by our mother leaving, our daddy still had to go to work. In the beginning, my two older sisters and I would take turns staying out of school to care for our two youngest sisters. This lasted for about a year until the neighbors started to notice, and soon, the welfare people showed up and took me and all my sisters to an orphanage.

The orphanage was more horrible than I had ever imagined. They put me in one room and one of my sisters in another room. I still remember hearing Jan, my baby sister, screaming for mama and me. They wouldn't unlock the doors to our rooms and only let us out until it was time to eat. Thankfully, we were there only about a month before the orphanage decided they wanted to adopt us out to different homes. On my mother's side, my grandmother was not about to let that happen, so she adopted all five of us to keep us together. *I pour my praise on Him.*

After already raising ten children, my grandpa was very skeptical, but grandma got her way. We all learned to adjust to our new life, and they loved us so much. After a while, my grandmother went back to work in a cotton mill. She worked the night shift from midnight to eight in the morning. She fed us, put us through school, clothed us, and took us to church. She also made us sing in the church choir whether we wanted to or not. I know God intervened in our lives and I am so grateful that we got to stay together. If we had been adopted out to separate homes, we might not have ever known each other.

At fourteen, my grandmother enrolled me in school. It was a Christian high school and was combined with Holmes Bible College. There were many rules, and I remember rule number twelve was that "there will be NO communication between the boys and girls. No talking. No touching. Not even smiling!" That did not stop me from liking a boy named Michael.

I had no idea that God was directing my steps toward my future husband at that point. It was LaVerne's first year there, as well. I didn't notice him at first because I liked Michael and LaVerne left for a year, but when he came back, he was sixteen, very tall, and so good-looking. By this time, Michael and I had broken up, and I started smiling at LaVerne after he continued flirting with me for a while. During the Christmas holidays that year, we talked my uncle Sonny into taking us to Paris Mountain in Greenville, South Carolina. That's where LaVerne wrapped me in his trench coat and kissed me! I have never been the same since that day.

Healing Actions

1. Don't be afraid to believe in the impossible.
2. Think about any miracles you've experienced in your life. Write them down to remember that God does exist.
3. Listen to your inner voice, the Holy Spirit. What is He saying? Obey what He tells you to do.
4. Read God's Word every day.
5. Spend time in gratitude each day. Start a gratitude journal.

CHAPTER 8

We've Got the Power

by Edith Tripp

I have given you authority to trample on snakes and scorpions and to overcome all the power of the enemy; nothing will harm you.

—Luke 10:19 NIV

Healing is available for everyone, but it is only manifested when you embrace it, believe it, and receive it.

—Edith Tripp

QUARTETS

I was eight years old when the Lord spoke to me in my spirit and told me I would marry an evangelist. I didn't even know what an evangelist was, and the man I was in love with wanted to be a singer.

We all went our separate ways when school ended, but LaVerne and I still liked each other. After Christmas 1963, LaVerne went to Oklahoma City, Oklahoma, to sing with a quartet. I was so heartbroken because I was afraid I would never see him again. I missed him so much and cried for several weeks. I listened to Ray Charles sing "I Can't Stop Loving You" while LaVerne was gone.

One Sunday night, January 19, 1964, LaVerne called me and told me he had an actual job singing in a quartet, and they were paying him. His next words were, "So, do you want to get married?" I was so young—only eighteen, about to turn nineteen—but I said, "Yes!" He later told me while we were apart, his daddy said, "You'd better marry that girl before someone else does."

LaVerne asked me if we could get married in the church in which I'd grown up. I replied, "I guess so." The following Sunday, we were married in the Church of God in Easley, South Carolina, and the church was packed. I think everyone came to make sure it was true. After the wedding, we headed to Chocowinity, North Carolina, where LaVerne was from, just long enough to have a wedding shower. Then we loaded up everything we had in our 1953 Ford and took off for Oklahoma City, Oklahoma.

When we got there, we moved in with the baritone singer in the quartet, Dale McCoy, and his mother, who was so sweet to me. We stayed with them for about a month, and then we got our own little apartment. It didn't last long, and soon we had to move back in with the McCoys because we couldn't afford to live on our own.

About six months later, a guy from Iowa called La-Verne and the guys in the quartet to see if they would move there. He said he would put them on his payroll if they would allow him to sing with them. They all said yes. I was three months' pregnant at this point and vomiting every day, but we still loaded up and moved to Des Moines, Iowa.

When we got there, we rented an apartment in a basement where the pipes were running into the ceiling. It was so low that LaVerne had to bend over to walk around, so we stayed in bed a lot, which we didn't mind because we were still in our "honeymoon" phase. Soon we were able to rent a nicer apartment, and we thought we had "arrived," except we didn't have any air-conditioning. We had a fan, at least, that I had bought with money I made selling magazines. Sometimes we would walk down to the corner drugstore, where they had air-conditioning, and eat donuts. I was growing bigger by the day, and we have never forgotten those months. They were very special to us.

We were not there very long before the money ran out for the quartet, and we had to move again. We packed up everything we had except our ironing board into a U-Haul and our 1953 Ford and moved back to North Carolina. (We left the ironing board on the sidewalk in front of our apartment.) We didn't have any brakes on the car, so we used the emergency brake to stop. Our seat in the front was loose; we would rock back and forth. My baby was already getting used to the feel of a rocking chair before he was ever in one! We had called my mom and asked her if we could use her eight-by-twenty-eight-foot trailer. We parked it behind LaVerne's parents' house and stayed there until our first son, Robb, was born. We were overjoyed by the birth of our first child.

After Robb's birth, we moved to Easley, South Carolina, my hometown, so LaVerne could start singing with a quartet called The Sierras. Most of the members were from Virginia and Tennessee, so we ended up moving to Bristol, Tennessee. We did a lot of moving during those years. Robb turned one year old while we still lived there and I remember how cute he was eating his cake. LaVerne started selling cars for a while to help make ends meet, but then he was offered a job with an insurance and burial company called Huff Cook. The head of the company started a television show for the quartet, but he had a run-in with one of the members and gave LaVerne a choice—he could stay with the company or leave the quartet.

LaVerne was making more money than ever before, and now we had a baby to care for, so it was a hard decision. LaVerne thought about it; he would rather risk being sixty-five and have nothing than to miss this opportunity. So, that made our decision for us, and after the quartet ended, we moved back to South Carolina. LaVerne started singing on the weekends with the Palmetto State Quartet until he talked them into letting him sing full-time.

We lived there for five years. I took a job at a sewing factory to help out and tried to put Robb at a preschool, but he couldn't adjust. After I dropped him off one day, the school called me and said, "Mrs. Tripp, we don't know what to do with your little boy. He will not quit screaming for his mom." I could hear him in the background saying, "I not want to go to skiddy schooo, I not want to go to skiddy schoo." I said, "Of course, I will be right there." When I picked him up, I asked him why he didn't like it. All he would say was, "I not go back to skiddy schooo." So my sisters helped take care of him.

Robb was five years old when LaVerne heard the Blueridge Quartet in Spartanburg, South Carolina, needed a lead singer, and after many conversations back and forth—they were thinking of their piano player singing lead for the quartet—he was able to convince them he was the man for the job.

I remember the day LaVerne and Robb came to get me at the sewing factory. When I got in the car, Robbie said, "Mom, you neber havva go back to stayon sewing in clothes again." We moved to Spartanburg, and our lives changed so much.

The Blueridge Quartet started singing LaVerne's songs, and the biggest was "I Know." He sang with them for seven years, they were very good to him, and while with them, he learned a lot about taking care of and dealing with the business side of music. During this time, he started drinking and doing drugs, though, which ended up taking control of his life. Through his family's prayers, the Lord began dealing with his heart.

One night, while he was on the road, he called me and said, "Edith, I've rededicated my life to the Lord." My heart jumped for joy. I had been praying so hard! He told me that a lady had come to his concert that night after God told her to go. She told LaVerne that as she sat there and listened to the quartet sing, a dark cloud hovered over the group, and then it centered in on him.

After the concert, he said someone came up and said, "Can I talk to you?" It was her. He told me that he knew in his heart that it had something to do with God, and any other time he wouldn't have listened to a stranger, but he knew this time he should. The lady told him about the dark cloud moving in over him, and she said, "If you don't give your life back to the Lord and stop running from Him, and instead do what He wants you to do, you'll be taking thousands of people to hell." He thought this lady was just trying to scare him.

That night the Holy Spirit started dealing with him. He laid in his bunk that night on the tour bus, and for the first time in a year, LaVerne talked to God. He told me he said, "God, if You are real and heaven is real and what I've been taught all my life is real, then let me know." The sweet presence of the Holy Spirit flooded him, and at that moment, he knew God was real. He told all the guys what had happened, and all of them but one accepted Christ.

After seven years with the Blueridge Quartet, La-Verne quit the group and went into ministry full-time a few months later. Praise the Lord; prayers were answered—or so I thought.

Healing Actions

1. You are the only person you can change. As for everyone else, all you can do is love them.
2. Build yourself up. Strengthen yourself by listening and reading God's Word daily.
3. Think of ways you can work on your spiritual walk. Don't wait on your partner or situation to change. Take the initiative to make a change in your own life.
4. Carve out time in your daily life to be with God.
5. Too many options can dilute your focus. Keep your eyes on Jesus, and He will always guide you.

CHAPTER 9

Healing Jesus

by Edith Tripp

The Spirit of the Sovereign LORD is on me, because the LORD has anointed me to proclaim good news to the poor. He has sent me to bind up the broken-hearted, to proclaim freedom for the captives and release from darkness for the prisoners, to proclaim the year of the LORD's favor and the day of vengeance for our God, to comfort all who mourn, and provide for those who grieve in Zion—to bestow on them a crown of beauty instead of ashes, the oil of joy instead of mourning, and a garment of praise instead of a spirit of despair. They will be called oaks of righteousness, a planting of the LORD for the display of his splendor.

—Isaiah 61:1–3 NIV

LaVerne's journey into full-time ministry work began in his car. First he hired a piano player, Carl Morris, who is still one of the most incredible guys we know; he now pastors a wonderful church in Florence, South Carolina. As the ministry grew, we bought a van and hired two more guys. Then we had enough faith and decided to buy a bus, and as we traveled and LaVerne shared his testimony, souls were saved everywhere we went.

After several years of touring with these guys, LaVerne felt that I should start traveling and singing with him, along with our twelve-year-old son, Robb, playing the drums. We had a second son, Terry, by now who was three years old, and our little family went on the road together. We hired another piano player and a bus driver named Barney. I still call him the brother I never had.

Things were going well in our lives. One night after appearing on the PTL Network in Charlotte, North Carolina, with Jim and Tammy Bakker, Dr. Paul and Jan Crouch, who founded Trinity Broadcasting Network, happened to be watching us. Jan reached out to a friend of ours to ask if we would come to California and join her on TBN. We didn't know anything about Trinity Broadcasting Network at that time. But she continued to insist that we come out and join her. LaVerne finally said, "If you book us for a week in churches out there, we will come." Our friend John Noseworthy did just that, and we headed out to California.

After just one night on TBN with Jan, hundreds of people were saved, and she asked us to come back on the show with her and her husband, Paul, the next night. We had the vision to see people born again, and many more were saved the next night while we were on the show. After the program, Jan and Paul talked to us about doing our own family program. They wanted us to host the *Praise the Lord* program every Friday night. We were overwhelmed and amazed that this was all happening.

We accepted, and after flying back and forth every Friday from South Carolina to California, they eventually asked us to move there. Moving to California was a huge step for us, bigger than anything else we had done before. Since we started using soundtracks, we only had one other guy with us, Barney, our bus driver. He agreed to go with us, and we all made the big move to California. By now, Robb was fifteen, and Terry was six. We were off on a great adventure.

One night on a program called *Behind the Scenes*, which Paul Crouch had created to talk about what was going on with TBN, he asked LaVerne and me to come on and talk about our move to California. We had decided to move there, but we didn't yet have a place to live. Paul announced that we were moving to join them in California and have our own show while we were on the show. Yet, we didn't yet have a home, and so if anyone was willing to donate a place, we would really appreciate it.

We received many calls and letters from people with offers. There was one special lady who called us and said she and her husband were separating. Her house was available until she wanted to sell it. We had looked at many places, and most of them were dumps, so we were very skeptical. But when we drove up and saw it, our mouths dropped open. To our surprise, the house that became our home was in Beverly Hills, California, only ten minutes from Disney Land. The house had 3,500 square feet, a big pool, a jacuzzi that could hold sixteen people, and flowers everywhere. We thought we were dreaming. We lived in that house for five years and recorded our TV shows. We were blessed to live in California for ten more years. Our family grew, our sons got married, and our grandchildren were born during that time. In 1994, we all moved to Nashville, Tennessee. We were all so happy.

LaVerne and I wanted our ministry to grow. Over the years, we have seen and heard through television that over a million people have given their hearts to Jesus. Praise God! During those years, although behind the scenes of our huge ministry and success, what appeared to be perfect was not so perfect. Those were some of the most horrific years of my life and the lives of our family. LaVerne and I have been married now for fifty-seven years. I tell people that we have had about forty good ones because for many years he was addicted to alcohol and drugs.

It started before our ministry grew so large. Over the years, he would repent and tell me repeatedly he would never do it again. I would hide the car keys from him, and if or when he got in the car, I would follow him to make sure he didn't get caught by the police, get in a wreck, or kill someone else. There was a period for two years that I slept with my purse so he couldn't get any money. Drugs affect the whole family, and it is a demonic force that wants to wear you down. But I loved him so much, and I knew the Lord had told me I would marry an evangelist and carry the Gospel to the world. The enemy tried to stop us, but I kept standing on God's Word for myself. I would not give up.

One day as I was praying, the Lord released me from my commitment to LaVerne so that I could tell him if he didn't get help, then I would not stay. I didn't want to be another divorce statistic, but your flesh can only take so much if your spouse is putting you through hell. I started hinting that I would leave him if he didn't get help, but LaVerne was so controlled by his addiction that he was willing to sell our home, split the money with me, and go live on the street until it ran out. I had enough, and when I had the courage to tell him that I was leaving him finally, he could see the "tiger" in my eyes and that I meant it.

He went into rehab for thirty days, got out, and was sober for sixty-six days, then started going to AA meetings. That first meeting was not like anything else we had ever been to, and I thought to myself, *Oh God, is this what we are gonna have to do for LaVerne to stay sober?* But let me tell you what God did. There were three guys at that meeting. When the meeting was over, they came up to LaVerne and told him they hadn't been to the meeting in about two years, but the Lord told them to come that day, and now they knew why. They told LaVerne they'd attended a Christian-based meeting across town, and that he should go to that one. I was so relieved. Those men and that group became our covering for years, and we learned so much from them. I used to believe that drug and alcohol addictions were outright sins. But I learned that for some people, it is a disease. Their minds are not at "ease," and a person has to take something to get relief. I learned we should not condemn if we have never been there ourselves because we don't know what that is like for someone else.

When LaVerne started healing, so did I. I brought things into our marriage I'd never dealt with from my childhood that I had packed deep inside me. I didn't realize it until I started talking one-on-one and in the group we had. I got honest with myself and realized I was still carrying my feelings about my stepfather. I always felt like he had taken my mother away from me. Unforgiveness, bitterness, fear—the list of what I experienced goes on. It got so intense for me that I started pounding on the refrigerator they had in the room in one session. I experienced tremendous relief and emptied all the emotional and mental trash I had compacted over the years of my life that day. Then I let God fill me up again. I had to let it all go, because if you are full of junk, pain, and brokenness, God cannot come in and do His great work inside you.

Finally, LaVerne was freed from the grips of addiction, and with all the help we received, there is no way it happened without the help of God. Completely grateful for his recovery and walking in the peace of the Lord, we faced another unforeseen challenge while still on the world stage of weekly television. Both of my sons were served divorce papers two weeks apart. Our entire family was being split in two. The sorrow, loss, rejection, anger, and countless hours of tears are impossible to describe. I had three grandchildren at the time, and the grief of knowing the pain my grandchildren were about to face was indescribable.

After everything I had already been through, from my childhood to my husband's addiction, this was the most heart-wrenching for me. This hurt the most. My two sons, whom I love so dearly, as well as my grandchildren, and the thought of their soon-to-be sorrow was unbearable. I had faced the trauma of my own parents' divorce, and knowing what my grandchildren would face brought up some of those very same emotions in me all over again.

We would still get on the bus during this season and go to minister. We were traveling almost full-time. It was one of the hardest things for me to do. I would lie across our bed in the tour bus praying and crying, knowing they were discouraged and heartbroken, and I couldn't do anything to help. You don't feel like facing anyone but God. I am so grateful He knows a mother's heart—I know those prayers paid off.

I would go into a church and pray and believe for another mother who was troubled and believing in her situation—giving to someone else out of what I needed. I'm here to tell you it works. If you're in a depression, give your time to someone else who is suffering from depression. If you're lonely, give it to someone who is shut in and can't get out. If you have money, give it to someone who doesn't have any. Don't stay inside yourself. Jesus said, *Go tell the good news about how I have set you free.* And apply one of the most important commandments in your life—that you love one another as He loves you.

Is healing for today? Absolutely *yes*. Not only does the Word of God say so, but I have experienced it over and over again for myself, as you have read in my story. Here is one more story from my life to verify what I believe.

In 2004, I was having a hard time breathing and couldn't talk at times without coughing. LaVerne and I were invited to go to Disney Land for a family reunion by a wealthy married couple who had received Christ while watching us on TV. They lived in Chili but were coming to the States to have a family reunion, hoping their family members would give their hearts to the Lord, and several of them did.

They gave us "the key" to Disney, and we could go and do anything we wanted while we were there. We were so excited. But while I was there, I started running a fever and could hardly breathe. When we got home, I went to the doctor, and he performed an X-ray and some other tests. He called me on a Friday and said, "Mrs. Tripp, I hate to tell you this, especially over the weekend, but you either have cancer or tuberculosis."

I handed the phone to LaVerne and told him he had to hear what the doctor was saying to me. If I had not had the Word of God in my heart, I would have had a breakdown. *Thy Word I have hidden in my heart that I might not sin against God...or not believe....* One doctor saw the X-rays and said I would be dead in three months, but I chose to believe the Word of the Lord. My test for tuberculosis came back negative. Praise the Lord.

I had biopsies taken to see if I had cancer. The doctor's office said they would call me with the results. I went home and waited. On the day they finally called me, one second before the phone rang to tell me my results, I felt led to pull out a promise card we had on the counter that the kids had been playing with. The card I picked out of that deck said: *"You will live and not die, but declare the works of the Lord"* (Psalm 118:27 KJV). Hallelujah! Not our works, but His.

My results were that there was no cancer. Praise God! The doctor told me I had a disease called sarcoidosis. It is the growth of tiny collections of inflammatory cells in different body parts. I had a few questionable lymph nodes under my arms that were painful, but that was eighteen years ago. *Thank You for the stripes You took on Your back for my healing. What a wonderful healing I received from Jesus.*

Healing Actions

1. Find someone else who is going through the same struggle you are and invest your time, talent, or treasure with them. Sow where you need a harvest.
2. Step outside of yourself and your concerns and help someone else.
3. Get rid of what's holding you back. Forgive yourself and others, and walk in love.
4. Find an organization you are passionate about and serve or see how you can get plugged in. Figure out what needs to change about yourself and then put your growth into action.
5. Write down every day what you are grateful for.

CHAPTER 10

The Woman Who Pressed In

And Jesus said, Somebody hath touched me: for I perceive that virtue is gone out of me. And when the woman saw that she was not hid, she came trembling, and falling down before him, she declared unto him before all the people for what cause she had touched him, and how she was healed immediately.
—Luke 8:46–47 KJV

Luke 8 tells the story about a woman who helped inspire this book. She was a woman who had been sick for a very long time. She had been bleeding for twelve long years. Her peers rejected her. She was not permitted into the city. She was out of options with no hope of a cure. She had been to every doctor and pursued every possible opportunity to be healed from this horrible disease with no success. She spent all she had with no hope in sight.

Now, we are not just talking about a health issue. We are talking about a financial issue, as well. I have often observed that when a second problem comes from an original problem, oftentimes it can be just as bad or worse than the original one. For instance, maybe you have a situation with raising your child, and that issue has now turned into a marriage issue, or your work issue has now turned into a mental health issue. No matter what, the devil is always out to glean the most destruction from every attack.

For the woman in the story in Luke, everything that could be thrown at her to break her in life clearly had been thrown. For twelve years, she had every opportunity to have a nervous breakdown, to kill herself, or choose never to see the light of day again, but something inside her drove her to keep going—something more powerful than she! I know this is not a popular message or, frankly, a popular Scripture, but Proverbs 24:10 says, "If you fail under pressure, your strength is too small" (NLT).

I know that no one wants to be told they are too weak. It is so much easier to blame God for all your problems. Play the "victim-pity" card to what has been dealt to you in the game of your life—or it is everyone else's fault that you cannot succeed because of what has been done to you. This is a game that can be played your whole life. The power you have is your choice about the situation you find yourself in and what you plan to do about it.

As I read the passage about the woman who bled, I looked between the lines and saw a woman who had everyone to blame, everyone to accuse, except herself— but yet, that is not what we see in her. We see a woman who must have assessed her situation and realized she could not change her circumstances. She could not change her doctors' reports, nor could she change her financial situation. She was the only person over whom she had any control, and the only person in the story she could control was herself. Here is a primary key to healing: Work on yourself.

You may be reading this and asking, What can I possibly do? How can I not be a victim and begin the journey of being victorious in my life? Yes, it is a journey, and I believe miracles happen every day. Still, sadly many will never begin the press to start their journey to victory.

Instead of playing the blame game and lying helpless in a bed of depression because of what you have lost or whom you have lost, change your focus. Put your attention on what you can work on and strengthen, or where you can build endurance. Shift your attention onto what you can do to become stronger through Christ and get out of your situation. That may sound selfish at first, but the only actual work we can do on ourselves is through the cross and what He did for us at Calvary.

You also have a voice, whether you believe it or not. Use it! What are you saying? What are you speaking over your situation, and most importantly, what are you saying to yourself about yourself? What do you know about yourself? In the text, where we read, "the woman" said to herself...*If I touch Him, I know*...consider this: What do you know? What truth do you know about yourself? What you KNOW is what you can change, what you can strengthen, and what you can redefine through God's Word.

Most people only know what others have projected onto them. In the story we are referring to, this woman was an outcast. I imagine she must have been told her life had no value, no hope for health, prosperity, or abundance for twelve years. In the same way, many of us only know what we have been told. Sadly, many people in their childhood never received affirmation or value. Then they become an adult and marry a partner who gives them no value or affirmation. The cycle continues, yet they believe there is more in their heart but they never take the time to find out for themselves who they really are in Christ.

One of the fantastic gifts about our Christian journey is that we have extraordinary power, and every believer has it. It is the power of choice. This woman in our story made a continuous decision to do something about her situation. She made a choice. Her will did not consider the most straightforward path or the simplest. Not even the path of least resistance, and she chose to leave where she was in the situation she found herself in. At that moment was the beginning of finding her healing, her miracle—she officially pursued and pressed forward with everything she had within her.

You will never leave where you are until you decide where you want to be. Did you know that 98 percent of Americans do not have written goals, nor can they say what they really want? How can you ever be healed if you don't even realize what kind of healing you need or desire?

Due to conditioning from childhood, peers, or the surrounding culture, some of you have been highly influenced to stop dreaming or believing. You've been beaten down in your life and never taught how to want more or that you deserve better. You begin saying your own negative self-fulfilling prophecy: *No one likes me. I cannot have that kind of car. I cannot make a difference in my city. I can't be healed. I don't deserve to be loved.* Guess what? You end up being right. You said it; you believed it. You choose it; you live it. Over and over again, you keep creating the same situations in your life. What you believe, you create.

A wonderful thing for each of us is that we have the power of choice and any of us can begin now to make new ones at any moment. Today is the day when life will be different because we are going to be different. Every moment is an opportunity for a new choice. Sometimes that means the simple act of how we choose to respond to a situation that has happened before. We have great power in that. Our silent thoughts can change our whole life in an instant, like the words that follow:

Though the woman who bled said no words out loud. All of heaven and all of hell heard everything she was saying--

I will not give up. I will not be denied. I am worth being healed, and God values me. No one in the crowd is more eligible than me for a miracle. This is my time to be healed, and I will not wait another day. The moment will not pass me by. I have waited long enough, I have spent enough, Jesus is enough. He is all I need; I know I will be made whole. I will touch Him, and I will be healed! I will not be stopped or cheated out of my miracle. Neither the crowd, nor the weather, nor the Law, nor the religious elders, will get in my way. I will get what I came for. No more delays. No more denials. Twelve years is long enough. Today is my day. I claim it now in the name of Jesus Christ.

Healing Actions

1. If you are having health issues and praying for healing or a miracle, you must move forward toward that healing with actions.
2. Strengthen your inner man through the Word of God daily.
3. Declare what God says about you and your situation until you know it.
4. Keep your eyes and thoughts focused on God and let Him lead you toward your healing.
5. Never give up or stop believing in your healing, whether it's emotional, mental, physical, or spiritual healing that you need.

Robb and Edith

Epilogue

She Was Healed is a book born out of a desire to help hurting people, but its focus is on women. As we sat around the kitchen table, Edith; my daughter, Hannah; and I had been discussing writing a book that would help women heal for months. One day while driving down the road it felt like the Lord spoke those three words to me: *She was healed.* I instantly called Edith and said, "I think I have the title for our book!" With her ever-encouraging voice, she replied, "I love it!"

Edith had been asked to write a book so often, but she always passed. To quote her, she said, "I never felt led." Then she would follow that and say, "But I'm going to write this book to help Hannah. I see the gift of writing in her, and I know God's going to use her writing gift. I am her grandmother. I want to help Hannah all I can. If my story helps others and gives Hannah an open door or an opportunity to share her gift, that is my gift to her." In 2021, coming out of the pandemic, we finally got the book proposal finished and had it in the hands of the publisher in the fall of 2021.

We are very excited about this book that is filled with powerful stories that Edith, Hannah, and I have experienced. The only way we overcame was through our faith, believing in God's Word, and pressing through. Even when we didn't think we could go on, we had to keep moving forward. Everyone has struggles, trials, tribulations, and the loss of loved ones. However, you can still overcome these things with the loving guidance and strength of Jesus Christ. Before this book went to print, our family lost my sweet husband, Robb, and his beautiful mother, Edith Tripp. We are still grieving, but we know they are both with the Lord together—that brings us all comfort, and we miss them every day.

In February 2021, my precious husband stepped on a screw at a box store and ended up having complications. Infection set up in his body, and he fought it all year. We thought it was gone, but it unexpectedly came back. Ultimately, my husband went into cardiac arrest on November 9, 2021. The doctors told me that the infection in his body had worn down his major organs and caused his heart to weaken, thus causing the cardiac arrest. He did not have any blockages or a heart attack.

We would then fight the biggest battle he or I had ever fought—the greatest fight of faith. During the first three days of his hospital stay, I literally stood beside his bed and interceded for his life. I would decree, "Robb Tripp, you and I are one flesh, and I say that this flesh shall live and not die."

We were in the hospital for thirty days. My husband was in the CCU. I had every prayer warrior around the world praying, and we saw results from our prayers. So many miracles happened, including his brain scans beginning to improve. The doctors told me this was a very "unusual occurrence." I had the most famous pastors and preachers in America texting me or calling almost daily. I had not one doubt in my mind that my husband would live. I was full of faith.

When he went into cardiac arrest, he did die, and they brought him back to life after seven rounds of CPR. After thirty days in the hospital, we could bring him home. I had twenty-four-hour nurse care. He was still not fully responding, but he was slowly beginning to come back to life. He had suffered brain damage, but the head neurologist said it happens to stroke and heart attack victims every day. It was still possible for him to fully recover. It all depended on him.

By faith I took him home knowing 100 percent he would be raised up; we had seen so many miracles already. I knew and believed the work would be finished at home. We had a nurse at the house with us, but he was not even home for a full twenty-four hours. On that

Wednesday, just twenty hours after coming home, he went to his heavenly home to be with Jesus. Robb had traveled the world. He was on worldwide television four times a week by the time he was fifteen. Robb was always going somewhere to make a difference. He made his final trip on December 8, 2021, at 2:02 p.m. My sweet Robb was only fifty-six years old.

In reflection, I believe my husband saw Jesus when he was in cardiac arrest, and I believe he chose to be with the Lord. It felt like Robb had stopped by the house and knew that everything was okay, saw that all was well, and then he went on to be with his Savior, knowing we would all be together in the morning. There is no time in heaven. So truly, in the morning, we will be together as though no time has passed.

I have not one doubt that my husband is with Jesus. I struggled with understanding how my faith had not been enough to see his ultimate healing on earth. I didn't get what I wanted, but Robb got his choice. This is where many people get stuck and can't get past the issue. They are lost in the questions of "why." Why did this happen? Why did I have to lose my loved one? I have since realized that the faith I was standing on, which I thought was for my husband, was actually for my children and me. The faith that I kept was my own, and it is what has sustained me.

On December 10, 2021, we laid my precious husband to rest. I was forty-eight years old. Our son was just sixteen years old and in high school, and our daughter had just turned twenty, still in Bible school. In a million years, I would never have dreamt I would find myself labeled with those horrible words, *widow* and *single mother*. How would I go on now? I had to press forward. I had two children who needed me, and it was essential for me to carry our life on for Robb and our family. At the same time, I knew this book, *She Was Healed*, was lying in our publisher's office taunting me. It was like the enemy was trying to take the book and beat me over the head with it. He was questioning me: *Are you gonna do something with it or not?* This book gave me a renewed purpose and mission to help others heal.

While trying to put the pieces of my life back into some version of living, two short months later, on February 17, 2022, my precious mother-in-love went home to be with her son Robb and her Savior. Everyone wants to know how she died or why she died. My mother-in-law with her husband, LaVerne, witnessed over two million documented souls come to Jesus. Her songs are known around the world. She went from an orphanage to what some would call a palace. She was the most loving, giving person I have ever known. If you knew her, you loved her.

Edith was diagnosed with a disease called sarcoidosis eighteen years before. She was given one year to live at that time, but she lived eighteen more! Praise the

Lord. Edith was a born fighter. I believe Edith fought every day to live in healing for those eighteen years, and after her son went to be with the Lord, she simply decided not to fight anymore. She was seventy-seven years old; lived an amazing, full, and prosperous life and was ready to go home. I still, without one doubt, know my mother-in-love believed Jesus was her healer. She spent her whole life telling people that "no one ever cared for her like Jesus." That is still her truth.

I know my husband chose to be with Jesus. I believe he knew and understood the rehabilitation he would be facing. There was no way he would be anything but his best in this life. He would never want to be a burden. Robb was a drummer, musician, producer, pastor, and a magnificent singer. He was the best father and most wonderful husband and provider. Robb was a born leader; his personality filled any room in which he found himself. People were drawn to him, and he was always the life of the party. He was a Grammy award winner and a world changer. He lived an amazing life, and the only thing he didn't live to see were the grandchildren that he mentioned so often—but my husband is an overcomer.

I believe we could've prayed all night until we were blue in the face, but my husband made a choice to go and be with the Lord. The one thing that God will never touch is man's will. You will never out-pray another person's will if they choose to go and be with the Lord. God honors man's free will. There's nothing you can do about it; that is how we get saved.

As I write these words to you, I'm sitting on my front porch, looking at the beautiful green grass. The sun is shining, and the wind lightly blows through the trees. I can hear the birds singing. This is the same porch that my husband and I would sit on and talk about how fun it would be to watch our grandchildren play with the dog in the yard someday. Today this porch feels different; even though the grass is green, it has a different shade. Even though life feels different, and looks different, I have to go back to what I know and where my life is now.

I remember the woman with the issue of blood in Luke 8:43–48. Life had not dealt her an easy card. Her desired result for a life of being whole was not just handed to her. She had to decide then to pursue that desire through pressing: pressing through her past, what others might do or say, pressing through her grief and sorrow of twelve years lost to sickness. The Bible says she had spent all she had. All her provisions were depleted. She had no rich husband at home. She was at the end of her rope. So, she did what I am now doing— thinking about what I know to be true and choosing to press. I know that Jesus is the Healer. I know that by His stripes I was healed; therefore, I am. I know my faith is enough. Everything has changed for me, but God never changes. I know I still have a future. My children will be what God has called them to be. The Word of God is still true, and I dare say, the best is still yet to come in my life. I am moving forward in my life, walking on faith, and pressing through.

I am forever grateful for the great love affair I had with Robb, and the nearly perfect marriage my husband and I had. Robb was the best husband. In twenty-one years of marriage, I never felt disrespected, unloved, or rejected. If you were with Robb Tripp, you were loved and cared for with excellence. Robb was always encouraging and inspiring. The sky was the limit. If Robb loved you, then you knew it. He had no problem expressing the love in his heart for others with words and deeds—that made him a rare man and so special. He was the best father, always mindful of his children. He declared God's Word and promises over them because he was a man of faith and not afraid to lead his family; he took pride in doing it. He was the head of his household and the leader of the family.

Edith Tripp was always the most wonderful mother-in-law, friend, cook, mentor, and encourager. Her giving spirit is truly unmatched. She walked in love like few I have ever known. She was and still is an incredible teacher for all of us. Edith was a rare soul who walked among us and shared her gifts. She has truly blessed me in my life.

As I look back, my only question is, did I enjoy the moments I had? Did I enjoy the journey? Did I enjoy the true gift of a beautiful life that is mine, or did I simply not realize how great life was. Believe me, I now know it was truly remarkable. From my childhood to the present, I have been so blessed. I'm so thankful for every moment, every song. I'm grateful for the music and every sermon I heard my husband preach and every time I heard him laugh—but as I sit here reflecting upon this book, *She Was Healed*, I know I cannot be a victim. I cannot fall into the grip of despair or allow the word widow to be my definition for the rest of my life.

Like our example, the woman in Luke 8, I refuse to be a statistic. I will not go into the grave with my husband, as much as my flesh would want to crawl in a hole and die with him. My children do not deserve to lose both parents. They have already had to put one parent in the ground, and I refuse to make them bury another, even if I keep breathing—I will not just breathe. I will live!

I could get mad at Robb for leaving us and thinking ahead of all the days he'll miss, like our daughter's wedding and our son's high school graduation. How will I feel when we have those grandchildren? I have to leave that with Jesus and know that God's grace is sufficient for that day. God's mercies are new every morning. So, I refuse to take on tomorrow's grief because tomorrow I will have a new grace for that day.

I have walked through days I would have never thought I could or would, having to face all the things that go with death: the expenses, estate taxes, walking into people's rooms and seeing the genuine sorrow on their faces and knowing that grief is for you. If you were having a good day for one moment, the look on their face quickly reminds you how sad your life is. Even though I am walking through the valley of the shadow of death in my life, I choose to say I will fear no evil, for I know that God is with me. I speak what I know is the truth and speak what I know to myself. God still has a future for me. Like the woman in Luke 8, I press in and grab the grit to keep pressing. She was healed. Isaiah 53 is the truth. I am healed, and I will be made whole.

My healing is hidden in my daily routine. So, I choose to get up every morning, read God's Word, and listen to God's Word. I take control of my thoughts. I focus on the goodness of God, and I am thankful for every moment that I've had with my husband and with my mother-in-law, like meals around the table. I reflect with joy on the Christmases, the vacations, every kind word. I am happy when I remember every time my mother-in-law told me, "You are a wonderful mother." I choose to rejoice. I know sorrow must go because joy always comes in the morning.

If you are reading this book. I hope you know that I fully understand that hard times come. Into every life, some rain must fall, but I still believe, and I still say that Jesus is the answer. There is hope because I have faith. I have also had an attitude adjustment regarding things that matter and things that don't. Take the time to enjoy your life. If you're in a good season, rejoice. If you're in a sorrowful season, know that joy will come again. Let the small stuff go, like if you burn your dinner, your child gets bubble gum in her hair right before church, or you don't have anything to wear to your next event. Don't let the small things steal your joy. Step back and realize that life is good. Live every moment of your life. It is your gift to enjoy.

This was the most challenging chapter of this book to write. It is challenging to put the finality of my husband's life, our marriage, and our ministry into a chapter that will have a final period on it. It's tough to accept that the woman known worldwide for her kindness, whom God allowed to be just for me, is gone, and I will never hear her voice again. I must somehow muster up the strength and the courage to keep *pressing* on.

Looking back at Edith's urgency to get her part of this book finished, I know that was the Holy Spirit, because He knows all things. He knew what was coming for Edith and that she genuinely wanted to see women made whole; all the more, she wanted her daughter-in-law and granddaughter to be healed.

I hope you can appreciate the cost of this book, meaning the expense of the experience of suffering and sorrows. Many great victories have been recorded as well within its pages. I pray you are encouraged by these stories. I promise I will, and I do, adhere to every suggestion in every chapter. I refuse to let the devil take me out. I have come too far to give up now. It is not what life brings you that matters; it is your response to it. See yourself in the Scriptures. Imagine yourself being that woman with the issue of blood. Yes, your "issue" may be named something different, but don't be afraid to admit you have an issue. And then, just like she did, you press and keep pressing until you have been touched, changed, renewed, revived, and healed! It won't happen if you quit. You can do it. So I encourage you to start here, and start now. Do not live another day in despair. Take the challenge and join the tribe of the healed. Read this book and apply the healing steps. Choose to be thankful and believe still that you can be healed and live the life you want to live. As for me, to this day, I still say this is my testimony: She was healed. I am healed!

Family Photo

Notes

These are Edith's final words and thoughts about her family, whom she loved so much:

Jesus has healed my family and me in so many ways, so many times. LaVerne has been sober for thirty years now. My prayers were finally answered: Both of my sons have gotten remarried to amazing, wonderful women of God, and all our grandchildren are living for and doing good works for the Lord. You must never give up, but keep speaking the words God has given us over everyone and every situation we face. His way and light are the only way.

My boys, Robb and Terry, are very different from each other, like most siblings. God gave them the wives who would help them each in the ministries they were called to do. Robb and Shanda pastor a wonderful church, The Fire Place Fellowship, in Hendersonville, Tennessee, and they have a global ministry. Robb has a recording studio and has produced many projects and anointed people over the years. He is an amazing drummer and has won a Grammy award. His wife, Shanda, has a heart for mission work and created the Love from Music City Organization. It is a nonprofit that serves the foster children, veterans, and orphans in Haiti. She has a weekly show called *Girl Sessions*, featuring stories and inspiring guests.

Their children, Hannah, now twenty, and Lawson, seventeen, are both serving the Lord. Hannah is studying in ministry school, and she is a terrific writer. I know we will see more from her. Lawson (our favorite and only grandson)—I call him "cutie"—is so smart, intelligent, and sweet. He plays the guitar and sings in the praise and worship team at his parents' church. When he preached his first sermon at church, we were there to "Amen" him. He did a great job. Maddie, my oldest granddaughter from Robb's first marriage, lives in California and is married to Jarod Moses, who is the youth pastor in their church. Maddie has a master's degree in nutrition.

Terry says he's been in the ministry life for forty-five years, and he's only forty-seven years old. He ministers and travels all over the United States, in big churches, in small churches, and now he goes into prisons. He is seeing great things happen with the prisoners, especially those who read his number-one bestselling book,

Shut the Hell Up. It's about shutting up the evil one who is talking to you and trying to destroy your mind. Terry has written many other books, and his latest is on the New Testament and Proverbs. It has his God-given empowerment sayings and what the verses are saying to him. He also has a thirty-minute TV show in Florida. His wife, Kim, travels with him sometimes, but she mostly stays home to teach their only daughter, Isabella. Kim is very crafty and always makes something for her friends or family. She is an entrepreneur and sells Lipsum lipstick and lip gloss, which I love.

Kim was told she could not have children, but she and Terry prayed, agreed, planted the seed, declared, and believed the Word of God for a child. Our Bella was born on LaVerne's sixty-first birthday. Wow, look what God did! Bella is a precious gift. She takes dance and voice and sings like an angel. She loves theater, wants to be a professional dancer, and loves math.

Rosebud is Terry's oldest daughter and our oldest, grandest granddaughter. When she was born, I was in the room, and I've never been the same. She is beautiful and loves life to the fullest and God with all of her heart. She lives in Texas and is married to Anthony Lewis. They own a dance studio and teach every age from ballroom to boot-scooting boogie. They love it and have two beautiful children—Marley is six, very dramatic like her mom, and she owns the room when she walks in.

Pierson is three, all boy, and he loves his mom, dad, and sissy. He is into *Toy Story* and calls LaVerne "Pop Boy." They love their Papa Terry, and Marley is glued to his side every time she is with him. Precious!

Lacey, Terry's other older daughter, lives in Canada with her husband, Nic Neustaedter, and they have two little girls, Eden and Shiloh. Our whole family would agree that Lacey is so special and loves the Lord and her family so intensely. She is one of the kindest, sweetest ladies you will ever meet. Her husband is the youth pastor at their church, and he does a wonderful job alongside Lacey. She helps Nic with buying houses and flipping them. They have been very successful at it. Their girls are getting their personalities, and LaVerne and I love FaceTiming with them and seeing them loving on each other. So cute.

I've told you all of this to let you know there is hope in Christ Jesus, who is our only Hope. I could keep telling you stories, but I want to tell you that whatever you are going through, whether it is a divorce, a health issue, or a drug or alcohol problem, nothing is too big for Him to handle. Find a Scripture that you love and stand on His Word. He promised us that our whole family could be saved, and we are a testimony of that. Your family can also be healed.

Edith's Family Recipes

These recipes are very special to our family, and our favorites Edith made with love. We wanted to share them with you and hope you will enjoy them as much as we have.

Served every holiday at the Tripp family table.

Edith's Million-Dollar Pie (the favorite "Elie" dessert of Lawson, Edith's only grandson)

5 lemons, juiced
1 can sweetened condensed milk
1 cup pecans
1 cup drained, sweetened strawberries
1 cup drained pineapple bits
1 16-oz. container of Cool Whip
Graham cracker or Oreo piecrust

Mix juice and sweetened condensed milk. Add fruit and nuts to the mixture. Add Cool Whip. Pour into prepared graham cracker or Oreo piecrust. Freeze for 2 hours.

Edith's Orange Jell-O Salad (Hannah Tripp's absolute favorite)

1/2 cup cottage cheese
1 box orange Jell-O
1 cup pecans
1 can drained pineapple
1 can drained mandarin orange slices
1 16-oz. container of Cool Whip

In large bowl, mix cottage cheese and dry Jell-O mix. Add drained fruit and nuts. Mix with Cool Whip. Enjoy. (You may substitute sugar-free Jell-O and Cool Whip to cut calories, if needed.)

Edith's Beef Brisket (Robb's favorite)

1 large beef brisket
1 jar chili sauce (you can find it near the ketchup
  in store)
1 packet Lipton onion dry soup mix
1 can Coke
1 sliced onion

Lay brisket in a large baking dish, fat side up.
Pour dry onion mix directly onto the top of the beef.
Pour chili sauce directly onto dry onion mix on top
of brisket.
Lay sliced onions on brisket.
Pour Coke into the pan around the beef. It should be
about an inch deep around the beef.
Cover with tin foil.
Bake at 350 degrees for 4 to 5 hours, depending on
the size of the brisket. Beef should be tender and pull
apart. You may cut it into portions and serve it on a
platter or straight out of the baking dish. The juice is
ready to use as gravy. It will taste more like BBQ than
traditional gravy. Men always love this dish. You can
serve a large group with very little effort.

About the Author

Shanda Tripp was born with a passion for helping those who are less fortunate. Her earliest memories are those of helping others. From foster children and orphans, Shanda's heart is to see hope restored to those who have lost hope. She founded Love from Music City to be a conduit that gives to those in need. LFMC has been instrumental in changing hundreds of lives and restoring hope to those in need.

Shanda is the cofounder and pastor of The Fire Place Fellowship in Hendersonville, Tennessee. Shanda enjoyed twenty-one beautiful years of marriage to her late husband, Grammy award–winning producer and pastor, Robb Tripp.

Robb and Shanda are the parents of two wonderful children. Hannah and Lawson Tripp. In addition to Shanda's world travels, she is a sought-after inspirational speaker and visionary. Shanda has a keen ability to inspire others to make a difference.